What Others Are Saying About
The Power of Prophetic

C000003827

Want to be more effective in prayer? Want to ma̲̲̲̲̲̲̲̲̲̲̲̲ ...... ̲̲̲̲̲̲̲̲ before the throne of God? Want to learn from a veteran champion and not a novice? Then go no further! Destiny is staring you right in the face through the life, ministry, and writings of Kynan Bridges. *The Power of Prophetic Prayer* will definitely increase the level of revelation in your life, give you strategic understanding of the practical how-to's of prayer, and propel you into prayers that strike the mark!

—*Dr. James W. Goll*
Founder, Encounters Network
International best-selling author

Kynan Bridges stirs up a passion and hunger within the heart of the believer to long for and to see the glory of God! In his latest book, *The Power of Prophetic Prayer*, Kynan prepares the body of Christ to get ready to see this all-powerful God work in our lives and manifest His glory and kingdom.

—*Dr. Jeremy Lopez*
CEO of Identitynetwork.net

Kynan Bridges is one of my favorite Bible teachers. We are on the precipice of the greatest revival and move of miracles in history. This book will "make sure" you fulfill your prophetic destiny.

—*Sid Roth*
Host, *It's Supernatural!*

Kynan's new book, *The Power of Prophetic Prayer*, teaches us how to pray strategically in accordance with God's word to get results. In this book, Kynan gives insight into his unique prayer methods that he has used through the years to transform not only his life, but the lives of countless others. Prophetic prayer is the right and the privilege of every believer. As you put the principles in this book into practice, watch and see how your life and all the lives of those who come into contact with you will be transformed.

—*Pastor Gloria E. Bridges*
Ministry Director
Grace & Peace Global Fellowship, Inc.

In his new book, Kynan Bridges takes the reader on a journey of discovering their God-given power. He combines Scripture with practical application from his own life stories, all while weaving prophetic prayers, insights, and practicums throughout the teaching. This book is a muscle-builder for those who want to transform their life and the lives of others through prophetic prayer!

—*Cindy Stewart*
Pastor, The Gathering, Tarpon Springs, FL
Author, *Believing God and Believing His Word*

Doleen Moore

KYNAN BRIDGES

THE POWER OF PROPHETIC PRAYER

WHITAKER
HOUSE

Unless otherwise indicated, all Scripture quotations are taken from the King James Version of the Holy Bible. Scripture quotations marked (AMP) are taken from are taken from *The Amplified* Bible, © 1954, 1958, 1962, 1964, 1965, 1987 by The Lockman Foundation. Used by permission. (www.Lockman.org). Scripture quotations marked (NKJV) are taken from the *New King James Version*, © 1979, 1980, 1982, 1984 by Thomas Nelson, Inc. Used by permission. All rights reserved.

Boldface type in the Scripture quotations indicates the author's emphasis.

All definitions of Greek words are taken from the New Testament Greek Lexicon—King James Version, based on Thayer's and Smith's Bible Dictionary, plus others (public domain), www.BibleStudyTools.com. All definitions of Hebrew words are taken from the Old Testament Hebrew Lexicon—King James Version, which is the Brown, Driver, Briggs, Gesenius Lexicon (public domain), BibleStudyTools.com.

Unless otherwise indicated, all dictionary definitions are taken from *Dictionary.com Unabridged*, Random House, © 2015.

THE POWER OF PROPHETIC PRAYER:
Release Your Destiny

Kynan Bridges Ministries, Inc.
P.O. Box 159
Ruskin, FL 33575
www.kynanbridges.com
info@kynanbridges.com

ISBN: 978-1-62911-622-8
eBook ISBN: 978-1-62911-623-5
Printed in the United States of America
© 2016 by Kynan Bridges

Whitaker House
1030 Hunt Valley Circle
New Kensington, PA 15068
www.whitakerhouse.com

Library of Congress Cataloging-in-Publication Data
Names: Bridges, Kynan, author.
Title: The power of prophetic prayer : release your destiny / Kynan Bridges.
Description: New Kensington, PA : Whitaker House, 2016.
Identifiers: LCCN 2015042850 | ISBN 9781629116228 (trade pbk. : alk. paper)
Subjects: LCSH: Prayer—Christianity. | Prophecy—Biblical teaching. |
  Prophecy—Christianity.
Classification: LCC BV210.3 .B737 2016 | DDC 248.3/2—dc23
LC record available at http://lccn.loc.gov/2015042850

No part of this book may be reproduced or transmitted in any form or by any means, electronic or mechanical—including photocopying, recording, or by any information storage and retrieval system—without permission in writing from the publisher. Please direct your inquiries to permissionseditor@whitakerhouse.com.

3 4 5 6 7 8 9 10 11   23 22 21 20 19 18 17 16

I dedicate this book to the Lord Jesus Christ, the King of Kings and Lord of Lords. I also dedicate it to Gloria Bridges—my lovely and virtuous wife, the mother of my four beautiful children (Ella, Naomi, Isaac, and Israel), and my number one supporter in life and ministry; I love you more than words can express. I could not have completed this book without your prayers and partnership. And to my church family, Grace & Peace Global Fellowship, who have been instrumental in praying for and supporting this project— God bless you!

Contents

Foreword

In 2012, the Holy Spirit expressly told me to make prayer my life's work. Of course, at the time, I didn't have the full understanding of what that meant—and I still don't see the full picture.

When He spoke those words to my heart, I had a sense that it meant teaching about prayer, writing about prayer, and engaging in ever-deeper levels of intercession. My first course of action was to pray for thirty days about what He meant, and then I launched a revival hub in South Florida that we call Awakening House of Prayer.

Any kind of faith-inspired prayer in the name of Jesus is effective prayer, but this concept of prophetic prayer that my friend Kynan unfolds in this book has been key in my life and ministry from the beginning. And I believe it can revolutionize your prayer life, too, if you'll fully embrace it.

As I talk with leaders around the country and travel to churches large and small, I have noticed a clear trend in the body of Christ. Jesus is stirring His bride to make intercession in an unprecedented way. I'm witnessing a "reset" of the prayer movement that thrills my heart. I believe the reason for this reset can be summed up in one word: revival. And I believe prophetic prayer is part and parcel of this reset in our own lives, in our families, in our churches, and across our nation.

Saint Augustine is thought to have once said, "Pray as though everything depended on God, and work as though everything depended upon you." Welsh-born minister and author Matthew Henry wrote, "When God intends to bless His people, the first thing He does is to set them a praying." John Wesley, a key figure in the Second Great Awakening, insisted, "God does nothing but by prayer, and everything with it." And D. L. Moody, an American evangelist and author argued, "Every great movement of God can be traced to a kneeling figure."

God wants to awaken your heart to His plans and purposes for your life, your family, your city, and even your nation. He wants to see revival spring forth in the hearts of those who have lost hope in an age of doom and gloom. He wants to reach a great harvest with His gospel of self-sacrificing love. Prayer is the baseline, the foundation, for all of this and more. And prophetic prayer, as Kynan lays out in this book, is an effective tool in the believer's hand.

Through prophetic prayer, God wants to share spiritual warfare strategies that will position you to overcome every enemy. Through prophetic prayer, God wants to help you gather the spoils of victory in this good fight of faith. Through prophetic prayer, God wants to lead and guide you into your destiny in Christ. If you've not seen the promised victories; if you've not experienced breakthrough prayer answers; if you've not entered into your purpose, prophetic prayer could be the missing link.

Prayer is essential in every believer's life, but prophetic insight throws fuel on the fervent, effectual prayer fire that James discusses in his epistle. You don't have to be a prophet to pray prophetic petitions. If you have the

Holy Spirit dwelling inside you, and a determination to see God's will come to pass in your life and in the lives of those around you, you are halfway to the answer. This book will equip you with the terminology and tactics you need to form and release prophetic prayers that get results. This is a must-read for every believer.

Jennifer LeClaire
Senior Editor, *Charisma* magazine
Director, Awakening House of Prayer
Author, *Mornings with the Holy Spirit*

Acknowledgments

First of all, I want to take a moment and acknowledge my precious Lord Jesus Christ. It is through Him that I am able to write this and all books. To my wife and ministerial staff, thank you! To my parents, James and Juanita Bridges—I honor you. To the Whitaker House staff, thank you for believing in me and helping me to release this message to the body of Christ. Special thanks to the production and editing team, including Christine Whitaker, Judith Dinsmore, and Jim Armstrong. Thanks also to many others, including Isheka Harrison (my staff editor).

I also want to acknowledge great men and women of the faith who have impacted my life and ministry in a positive way, either directly or indirectly, including Pastor Wayne C. Thompson, Dr. Mark Chironna, Derek Prince, Smith Wigglesworth, John G. Lake, Oswald Chambers, John Wesley, Jack Coe, Oral Roberts, Kathryn Kuhlman, R. W. Shambach, Kenneth E. Hagin, Dr. T. L. Osborn, Dr. Martin Luther King Jr., Heidi Baker, Bill Johnson, Randy Clark, Mahesh and Bonnie Chavda, Hank and Brenda

Kunneman, Apostle G. Maldonado, Sid Roth, Rabbi Jonathan Bernis, Dr. Cindy Trimm, Apostle Charles Ndifon, Dr. Charles and Francis Hunter, Joan Hunter, Pastor Marlin D. Harris, Dr. E. V. Hill, Dr. Barbie Breathitt, Mike Bickle, Pastor Andre Mitchell, Marilyn Hickey, Pastor Tony Kemp, John Loren Sandford, Dr. T. L. Lowery, Dr. Douglas Wingate, Benny Hinn, and Evangelist Reinhard Bonnke. Thank you for your service and gifts to the body of Christ.

Introduction

Prayer is one of the most powerful forces in the earth. Prayer invites eternity to invade time. Prayer can alter the very course of history, and reshape the world around us. Through prayer, we access the throne of grace. Prayer is absolutely amazing!

But if praying is so powerful, why do believers do so little of it? The answer is quite simple, actually; most people don't pray the way God has ordained because they don't know what prayer really is. And because they don't know, people inevitably reject their responsibility to pray and are therefore unable to reap its divine benefits.

You may be thinking, *Are there really divine benefits? What is the power and significance of prayer? Can I really manifest the miraculous through prayer and intercession?* These questions will be answered in this book. You are about to embark on a supernatural discovery of epic proportions. As you read the pages of this book, the Holy Spirit will alter the way you see prayer—forever! You are going to realize that prayer is more than a religious exercise; it is the supernatural catalyst that enables us to experience the power and presence of God in every area of our lives. We are not spiritual pacifists waiting on our lives to change while we hope for the "sweet by-and-by." No, we are priests and emissaries who have been ordained and empowered to release the kingdom of God in the earth, and thereby transforming the very course of our destinies, as well as the destinies of those around us.

Many of us may have heard of the terms "prophetic preaching," "prophetic teaching," or even "prophetic evangelism." But have we heard of "prophetic prayer"? What does that term even mean? Well, before we can answer that question, we must take a closer look at the meaning of prophecy.

Prophecy is defined as the function or faculty of prophesying or telling the future. In essence, prophecy is the foretelling or forth-telling of a divinely inspired message, typically communicated by a prophet. In recent years, we have been exposed to much teaching and writing on what is commonly known as "the prophetic." And yet, despite the fact that it is embraced by more people today than it was, say, twenty years ago, there is still widespread misunderstanding on the nature and function of prophets within the body of Christ. The goal of this book is not to convolute your knowledge of prophecy any further, but to reveal the relationship between prayer and prophecy and to show how relevant this spiritual tool is to every single believer.

What if I told you that the power to change your future was in your hands?

What if I told you that the key to your personal destiny, as well as to the collective destinies of those you love, was literally in your mouth?

What if I told you that the change that you have been so desperately seeking is *only one prayer away*?

1

The Power and Purpose of Prayer

And he spake a parable unto them to this end, that men ought always to pray, and not to faint.
—Luke 18:1

Prayer changes things!"

Growing up in the church, I heard that phrase early and often. Every Sunday, one of the old ladies in the church would tell you that she was "keeping you in prayer." What in heaven did this really mean? I hadn't the slightest idea, but it sounded really spiritual, so I appreciated the gesture. After a while, I picked up the lingo and joined in. I learned to mimic my environment and to regurgitate all the spiritual language that was expressed by the "deep" people in the church.

But over the past several years, the Holy Spirit has challenged me in ways that I can't begin to describe and the experience has prompted in my soul all sorts of questions about prayer. Is prayer simply something that religious people do out of a sense of obligation? Or is there more to prayer than meets the eye? Has God already make up in His mind what He is going to do in any given situation, or can prayer affect the outcome of our destinies?

I believe you are going to find, in the pages of this book, answers to questions you have been asking your entire life. You will discover the true biblical meaning of prayer (more specifically, prophetic prayer) and the divine power that prayer contains to change the very fabric of the world around you. You will discover that God has given you the most powerful tool in the universe, and you will learn how to use this divine tool to become everything God has ordained you to be.

More than a Religious Ritual

Prayer is an inescapable reality for every born-again believer, yet most born-again believers are not aware of the supernatural power and true spiritual significance of prayer. Not only that, but many believers don't realize the prophetic DNA that they carry, or the potential of this prophetic nature to alter the way we pray—forever! It's time for that to change!

During the time of Jesus, prayer was a very common practice. The Jews and the Gentiles alike followed well-established rituals for prayer. It was common for people in ancient times to invite divine intervention into their lives through the means of prayer. Even our Lord lived a consistent lifestyle of prayer. Why? In the eighteenth chapter of Luke, Jesus told a parable to His disciples to illustrate the power and purpose of prayer:

> *And he spake a parable unto them to this end, that men ought always to pray, and not to faint; saying, There was in a city a judge, which feared not God, neither regarded man: And there was a widow in that city; and she came unto him, saying, Avenge me of mine adversary. And he would not for a while: but afterward he said within himself, Though I fear not God, nor regard man; yet because this widow troubleth me, I will avenge her, lest by her continual coming she weary me. And the Lord said, Hear what the unjust judge saith. And shall not God avenge his own elect, which cry day and night unto him, though he bear long with them? I tell you that he will avenge them speedily. Nevertheless when the Son of man cometh, shall he find faith on the earth?* (Luke 18:1–8)

This parable teaches the importance of persevering in prayer. But I believe there is even more to this parable than you may realize. Notice that the Bible says the woman besought the judge to avenge her of her adversary. The word for "adversary" (*antidikos* in the Greek) in this particular passage means an opponent in a lawsuit. In other words, this woman was seeking vindication in a legal matter.

Why is this significant to our conversation about prayer? Because Jesus was teaching His disciples that prayer is more than a religious ritual; it is, in fact, a *legal transaction* that is recognized in heaven. This is why the woman went before the *judge*. Prayer is not just about comfort and healing. When practiced according to the Word of God, prayer initiates legal action in the courts of heaven, which affects the outcome of matters in the earthly realm. In essence, prayer avenges us of our spiritual adversary: the devil!

PROPHETIC PRAYER, WHEN PRAYED IN FAITH, IS A COVENANT TRANSACTION BETWEEN US AND GOD!

When we look at prayer from a legal perspective, it will change the way we approach prayer forever. We will recognize its profound power! In any legitimate court, the law recognizes whatever the judge decrees. The woman in this particular parable was seeking vindication. What is meant by the term "vindication"? Often, when we think of vindication, we think of someone being paid back for a wrong they have done or of some other form of retribution. From a biblical standpoint, however, vindication goes much deeper. The Greek word for "vindicate" (or "avenge") is the word *ekdikeo* which means to retaliate, to punish, to do one justice.

In a biblical sense, prayer is about the manifestation of God's justice in the lives of His children. By justice, we mean the purpose, intent, and will of God being realized in our lives; justice is the act of setting something in order, or making something right. The woman in the parable was seeking justice. She was imploring the judge to set things right on her behalf. This is the purpose of prayer! Every time we pray, we are inviting God, the righteous Judge, to reconcile every situation and circumstance in the natural realm with His will and purpose in the heavenly realm. Therefore, prayer is not just a religious act; it is a binding legal transaction.

So, when those women at my home church were praying for me as a young boy, they were essentially inviting God to reconcile every area of my life to His divine purpose. They were asking for everything that was misaligned, chaotic, and sinful, to be restored and made right by the power of the Holy Spirit.

You have probably never looked at prayer from this perspective. What would happen if you and I had a revelation of the legal/covenantal ramifications of prayer? I believe it would cause us to pray more confidently and consistently, knowing that the righteous Judge in heaven hears our every cry.

The Necessity and Power of Prayer

Throughout the Bible, we see God's power being displayed in the affairs of men by means of prayer. We see prayer exemplified in the book of Genesis when Abraham seeks God's intervention in the life of his nephew Lot. We see prayer demonstrated in the life of Jacob when he asks God to reconcile his broken relationship with his brother Esau and to deliver him from death. We see supernatural prayers in the book of Exodus, when the children of Israel plead for God's hand of deliverance from the oppression of Pharaoh. We also see prayer exemplified in the life of our Lord Jesus Himself in the New Testament. These are just a few examples that point to this reality: prayer is both biblical and necessary.

Why? What makes prayer God's preferred means to bring about change in the earth? First of all, we must recognize that God is a spiritual Being. The Bible tells us in John 4:24, *"God is a Spirit: and they that worship him must worship him in spirit and in truth."* In other words, God is spiritual; therefore, the only way that we can commune with God is by the spirit. Prayer is the spiritual mechanism by which we commune with God and invite His presence and power into our lives and into the lives of those we care about. This means that prayer is not optional; it is absolutely necessary. When Adam and Eve fell in the garden of Eden, they died spiritually and were cut off from sustained fellowship with their Creator. Ever since that time, the only way for mankind to connect with God has been through prayer and intercession. This is the reason Jesus said, "Men ought always to pray!" (See Luke 18:1.)

PRAYER RELEASES THE ATMOSPHERE OF HEAVEN INTO THE EARTH.

One day, many years ago, I realized that I owed a substantial amount of money that I could not pay. As with many situations before this, worry began to set in. There was no solution in sight. What on earth was I going to do? I walked out of the library and got into my car, and then suddenly felt the unction of the Holy Spirit to pray about it. As I prayed, I heard the voice of the Holy Spirit say, "Look on your dashboard!" I looked and saw an unfiled tax return from a year or two earlier. The next day, I took the tax return to a filing company and used the funds to pay off my debt in full. Glory to God! Now, this story may not seem like a major breakthrough or victory to you, but for me it was a monumental blessing.

The thing to note is the power of prayer in bringing about a change for the better. What would have happened if I had neglected to pray? What blessing would I have missed out on by refusing to invite God's divine intervention into the situation? We must remember that heaven has all the answers and resources we will ever need. Every time we pray we are inviting the atmosphere and power of heaven to invade our lives.

The concept of vindication is so profound when we realize just what we are asking God to bring into our lives. By praying about the circumstances of our lives, we are, in a sense, inviting God to bring His righteous vindication into the various situations that we face. Whether we are praying about healing, finances, emotional distress, or the salvation of a loved one, God is seeking divine opportunities to invade our lives for His glory, and to bring reconciliation, restoration, and vindication to any and every area of our lives.

The Holy Spirit: The Agent of Prayer

If God is the righteous Judge of all the earth, and heaven is the courtroom of the universe, then how do we know what and when to pray? How can we be sure that we are praying for the right things and are praying the right way? Surely *what* we pray about is of supreme importance. And it may be more organic than you realize.

Some people believe that in order for God to take our prayers seriously, we must always be praying about some geo-political issue, a global economic crisis, or ending world poverty, but the truth is that God is concerned with *every* aspect of our human experience. He cares about what is going on in our communities. He cares about what is taking place in our culture. He cares about our marriages and our families. He definitely cares about what is going on in our churches.

Psalm 9:4 reads, *"For thou hast maintained my right and my cause; thou sattest in the throne judging right."* We see again that God is the One pleading our cause in heaven, and acting on our behalf in the earth. The average person is not well-versed in matters of early law, so he or she needs the help of an expert. In every court, then, there are those who help us to navigate the complex landscape of the law, and who are able to represent us in legal matters. These experts are often referred to as lawyers or advocates and act as our agents in the courtroom. In the same way, the Spirit is our advocate, our agent, in the heavenly courtroom. As the Bible says, *"Likewise, the Spirit also helpeth our infirmities: for we know not what we should pray for as we ought: but the Spirit itself maketh intercession for us with groanings which cannot be uttered"* (Romans 8:26). The Greek word used for "help" is *synantilambanomai*, which means "to lay hold along with," "to strive to obtain with others," and "to help in obtaining."

Remember, we said that prayer is a divine legal transaction recognized in heaven. If prayer is a legal transaction, then it stands to reason that we need legal advocacy when we pray. In other words, the Holy Spirit acts as our supernatural Agent who assists, helps, strives with, and empowers us in matters of prayer.

THE HOLY SPIRIT PROVIDES SUPERNATURAL HELP TO THE BELIEVER IN PRAYER.

If we are honest, we can admit that when it comes to prayer, there are many times when we have no idea what to say or how. I remember the first all-night prayer session I attended at my church. I had never even heard of all-night prayer, much less participated. I vividly remember the pastor telling us it was time to pray. After the first hour, I ran out of things to pray about. Once I'd exhausted my list of immediate family members and friends, I really didn't have anything left to pray for. It was in that moment that I learned to rely on the Helper (that is, the Holy Spirit). I began to pray by the Spirit, and God started to reveal things I hadn't known about specific people and situations. Then, the Holy Spirit began to teach me how to pray for these people and situations.

What an amazing experience! Ever since that time, I have been learning to rely more and more on the Holy Spirit in prayer. He is the Agent of prayer! *"But the Helper (Comforter, Advocate, Intercessor—Counselor, Strengthener, Standby), the Holy Spirit, whom the Father will send in My name [in My place, to represent Me and act on My behalf], He will teach you all things. And He will help you remember everything that I have told you"* (John 14:26 AMP). Every time we pray, the Holy Spirit is literally searching the mind of God the Father to ensure that we are praying according to His will. If this seems too mysterious to you, then simply pray according to the Word of God and be assured that the Holy Spirit will take care of the rest.

The type of prayer we lift to the Father will vary, as we will discuss in greater detail later on in this book. However, all prayer has three things common: (1) It has a prophetic element; (2) God is glorified; and (3) Our lives are transformed. When I discovered the secrets to praying prophetically (that is, according to the will of God) my life was changed forever. I believe that your life is about to change forever as well!

Treasures in Earthen Vessels

If you are faced with a difficult decision and know that you're in need of divine guidance, where would that wisdom come from? Will you register for the latest seminar or conference, hoping it will offer the wisdom that you need? Will you collect a bunch of fortune cookies at a Chinese restaurant? Or will you expect the Holy Spirit to speak to you in a clear, concise way? The Bible tells us, *"For God, who commanded the light to shine out of darkness, hath shined in our hearts, to give the light of the knowledge of the glory of God in the face of Jesus Christ. But we have this treasure in earthen vessels, that the excellency of the power may be of God, and not of us"* (2 Corinthians 4:6–7). The word *"treasure"* in this passage is the Greek word *thēsauros*, which means "the place in which good and precious things are collected and laid up." It is literally a treasury or repository.

THE HOLY SPIRIT GIVES US UNLIMITED ACCESS
TO THE FATHER.

I want you to imagine for a moment that you are a treasure chest or vault, and the treasure inside of you is the Spirit of God. Because the Holy Spirit is omniscient and lives inside of the believer, the answers to our prayers will usually flow from *within* and not from the outside. The moment we became born again and received the Holy Spirit, we became God's treasure chest—full of His power, anointing, and revelation.

But how do we access the contents of that vault? In order to access a valuable treasure on earth, you would need a key or access code. And prayer is the spiritual key or access code that unlocks the treasures of wisdom, revelation, and knowledge—treasures that are already inside every believer via the Holy Spirit.

Many years ago, I was employed by a company that did contract work for the government. Because of the sensitive nature of what we did, every employee was issued a secure access badge that allowed us to enter and leave the building. Without this badge, an employee could not enter the workspace. After working for this company for quite some time, I decided to resign. Several months later, I went to visit some of my former coworkers and realized that I still had my access key in my possession. I suspected that the key no longer worked, but I decided to try it out, anyway, and see if I could enter the building. Sure enough, it didn't work. The system had automatically deactivated my access key when my employment was terminated.

PRAYER IS A SUPERNATURAL ACTIVITY THAT PRODUCES SUPERNATURAL RESULTS.

In a similar way, prayer is our spiritual access key to the things of God. Unlike the key card that I described, the access that the Holy Spirit grants us in prayer is supernatural and unlimited—it can never be "deactivated." In other words, our spiritual access key is not temporary or circumstantial, but a 24/7 access to the Father by the Holy Spirit. This is why the Bible tells us: *"For through him* [Jesus Christ] *we both have access by one Spirit unto the Father"* (Ephesians 2:18). Every time we pray in faith by the name of Jesus, we are accessing the heavenly realm. This access cannot be denied! Unfortunately, many believers are not aware of the supernatural access that they possess in Christ. What if, through prayer, we could receive supernatural downloads from God in prayer that would change our lives? What if we could walk in divine wisdom on a daily basis?

A believer without a prayer life is like an employee without an access key. No matter how awesome the resources behind the door, we cannot benefit from them unless we have the proper key. In the same way, when we don't exercise our spiritual privilege of prayer, we deny ourselves the rich blessings, benefits, and breakthroughs that God has reserved for us.

God wants us to experience supernatural results to prayer. He wants us to receive the wisdom and revelation that we need in order to live victoriously. If we are to walk in victory, we must practice a lifestyle of consistent prayer and communion with God. For the record, prayer is not a suggestion; it is a command from God! First Thessalonians 5:17 exhorts us, *"Pray without ceasing."* The beauty is that God never commands us to do something that does not bring blessing and prosperity into our lives. In fact, to the born-again believer, prayer should be as easy as breathing! We were created to commune and fellowship with God, and we have been given the grace to pray consistently and constantly.

What area of your life could use divine results? Have you prayed about it? If you are ill, you usually go see a doctor. If you are having problems with your taxes, you would probably talk with your accountant. If you were in a legal bind, you would consult your lawyer. Why is it, then, that when we need wisdom, knowledge, or understanding, we neglect to go before our heavenly Father in prayer?

Prophetic Prayer

Father, in the name of Jesus, I thank You for who You are and all You have done. Right now I decree and declare that I have perfect fellowship with You. I have a prosperous prayer life. In accordance with 1 Thessalonians 5:17, I pray without ceasing. I receive divine answers to my prayers. I love to pray and spend time with You, Father. I delight myself in prayer. Prayer is the priority of my life. As I pray, I hear specific insights and instructions for my life and the lives of those around me. I pray with both the Holy Spirit and my own understanding. Every time I pray, my prayers are answered in the name of Jesus Christ. Amen.

Prophetic Insights

1. How will viewing prayer as a legal transaction affect the way you pray?

2. Who is our agent and advocate in the heavenly courtroom?

3. How can we possess spiritual access to the blessings of God's kingdom?

2

The Spirit of Prophecy

And I fell at his feet to worship him. And he said unto me,
See thou do it not: I am thy fellowservant,
and of thy brethren that have the testimony of Jesus: worship God:
*for the testimony of Jesus is the **spirit of prophecy**.*
—Revelation 19:10

As we have discussed so far, prayer is essential for every believer. The Bible makes it quite clear that prayer is a supernatural tool capable of transforming our world. We know that prayer is communion with God. We also know that prayer is a spiritual, legal transaction that brings about God's righteous justice in the earth (that is, healing, deliverance, salvation, restoration, and so forth). However, I believe that prayer is even more than that! Let me explain.

Years ago, I was introduced to the prophetic movement. When I became born again, in the early nineties, one of the first spiritual gifts I was exposed to was the gift of prophecy. Every Sunday at the church I attended, the pastor would give a prophetic utterance. In addition, the pastor, as well as several other people, knew things about me and other individuals in the congregation that no one had told them. I soon learned that they had learned these things through what is called a word of wisdom, or a word of knowledge. I found this to be fascinating! I started asking questions, such as, "What is prophecy?" "Why is it important?" "What is the connection between prophecy and prayer?"

The word *prophecy* comes from the Greek word *prophēteia*, which means "a discourse emanating from divine inspiration and declaring the purposes of God, whether by reproving and admonishing the wicked, or comforting the afflicted, or revealing things hidden; especially by foretelling future events." Oftentimes, when we think of prophecy, we think of someone foretelling a future event; but that is only one aspect of prophecy. The key term in the definition of *prophecy* is "divine inspiration." Throughout the Bible, prophets delivered divinely inspired messages from God, usually with the theme of repentance, rebuke, restoration, or revelation. From Abraham to Malachi, the prophets of the Old Testament revealed the mind and purposes of God to His people.

PROPHECY IS MORE THAN THE FORETELLING OF THE FUTURE; IT IS ALSO THE CALLING FORTH OF THE WILL OF GOD INTO MANIFESTATION.

In the New Testament, the spirit of prophecy is manifested as more than divine inspiration—it is also supernatural testimony. The word "testimony" in the New Testament comes from the Greek word *martyria*, which means "a testifying; the office committed to the prophets of testifying concerning future events." The term *testimony* is often used in legal discourse and is defined as "evidence, a solemn declaration usually made orally, by a witness under oath."

Remember that we said that God is the righteous Judge of the universe. Well, consider now how every court of law responds to testimony.

Revelation 19:10 tells us that the testimony of Jesus Christ is the spirit of prophecy. The moment we were born again, we received the divine testimony of Jesus, which is the internal witness of His death, burial, and resurrection. This is the reason we are able to affirm without a doubt that Jesus is alive, because the Holy Spirit bears witness, or testifies, to the reality of Jesus in our lives. (See John 15:26.) The Holy Spirit lives inside us and testifies of the presence, power, and nature of God within. In essence, prophecy is the divinely inspired testimony of Jesus. Therefore, every born-again believer possesses the spirit of prophecy. You may not have thought of yourself as a prophetic person. But if you are, indeed, a believer in Jesus, you possess a prophetic nature—something we will discuss in greater depth later on. This prophetic nature enables you to release the mind and purpose of God in the various circumstances of your life.

Again, what does the prophetic have to do with prayer? Well, every time you pray or intercede for someone, you are drawing from the prophetic reservoir in your inner being. You are releasing a prophetic utterance over that person's future. You are calling the will and purpose of God into being in the life of that individual. This is an amazing reality many believers have yet to explore. What if God desired to use your prayers to manifest Himself in the lives of the people around you? Well, He does!

The Delivery Room

Many years ago, when my wife was about to give birth to our first child, we had a very difficult time. Our unborn baby was healthy, but my wife was experiencing several complications. She wasn't dilating at all, and since the doctors did not want our child's birth weight to be too high, they decided to induce my wife's labor at the risk of having to perform a C-section. Prior to this point, my wife had decided that she did not want to undergo a C-section. Yet the doctors informed her that the likelihood of her having to undergo the procedure was extremely high. After being in labor for several hours, my wife still showed little signs of dilation. I thought, *What are we going to do? How can we possibly avoid the operating room? Maybe it isn't God's will for her to have a natural birth!*

My wife had been praying for hours and was extremely exhausted. The doctor told us that if my wife was not ten centimeters dilated within the next hour, a C-section would be necessary. At this point, I began to pray earnestly. Led by the Spirit, I placed my hands on my wife's abdomen and prayed over her. Then, an interesting thing happened. I transitioned from praying that my wife would dilate to prophesying over her womb. I began to call forth my child. I commanded my wife's body to respond to the Word of God. I said, "Listen here, baby! Mommy and Daddy are waiting for you; it's time for you to come out, in Jesus' name! Listen here, cervix; it's time for you to respond!" Several minutes later, the nurse came into the room to check on my wife. To our amazement, she screamed, "The baby's head is coming out!" She told me to come and help, and I ran to assist with the delivery. Apparently, my wife had gone from two centimeters to ten in a matter of minutes. Praise God! We went from preparing for a C-section to having a natural birth in a matter of minutes, and a beautiful eight-pound baby girl was quickly born!

What happened? What changed? In the delivery room, I tapped into the spirit of prophecy and called forth a healthy delivery into manifestation. What would have happened if I had accepted the doctor's report as an unchangeable reality? I would not be sharing this testimony today!

God wants to give you a supernatural testimony of His power and goodness in your life. All you need to do is learn to tap into the spirit of prayer and prophecy.

EACH BELIEVER HAS A PROPHETIC DNA;
THEREFORE, WE MUST LEARN HOW TO ACTIVATE
THE WILL AND PURPOSES OF GOD
THROUGH SPIRIT-LED PRAYER, INTERCESSION,
AND DECLARATION.

Birthing the Prophetic

While my wife was giving birth to a physical baby, I was giving birth to something supernatural. I tapped into another dimension in prayer. Before this, my prayer life had been somewhat passive; I would pray the Word of God and wait for something to happen. If that "something" didn't seem to happen right away, I became discouraged. Little did I know that God was trying to birth something greater on the inside of me. The physical delivery my wife and I experienced was a prophetic symbol of the spiritual delivery that every believer must go through if they want to see supernatural results born in their lives. In essence, the prophetic is not obtained; it is birthed!

You already have the spirit of prophecy on the inside of you. Now, you simply need to learn to release that prophetic potential. Every challenge or difficulty we face is an opportunity for the power of God to bring change to our lives. The problem is that we rarely view the difficulties we face as opportunities. Instead, we tend to view them as liabilities. In other words, when we endure pain, hurt, disappointment, delay, or denial, we often allow the physical reality to limit us or to determine the outcome.

Remember, nothing can be birthed in the natural world without pressure. In the same way, the fruits of prophecy are always birthed in the place of pressure. The beauty of the Holy Spirit living inside the believer is the truth that He transcends any natural limitation we may face. The same Spirit that raised Jesus from the dead dwells on the inside of us! (See Romans 8:11.) And if the all-powerful Holy Spirit lives in us, then we ought to approach prayer with great boldness and confidence, knowing that the Creator of the universe is on our side! Instead of accepting defeat or despair, determine what the will of God is concerning your particular situation, and then declare it with all your heart. If you haven't yet discovered what God's will is, then go back to His Word! His Word is always His will.

IF YOU DON'T LIKE THE WORLD YOU LIVE IN,
CHANGE IT! PRAYER IS THE CATALYST FOR CHANGE.

The days of passive Christianity are over! We are living in a season in which God is raising up an army of prophetic people who will abandon the status quo and seek God with all their hearts. It doesn't matter whether you are a carpenter, a lawyer, a homemaker, a business executive, or a college professor, God wants to reveal Himself to you in the secret place of prayer and to use you to bring about His desired change in the earth. You may not have thought of yourself as an agent of change, but that is exactly what you are.

Prayer is the divine catalyst for change! The more we understand the purpose and power of prayer, the more we will be positioned to see God's will come into manifestation. As David said in the Psalms, *"But as for me, my prayer is unto thee, O LORD, in an acceptable time: O God, in the multitude of thy mercy hear me, in the truth of thy salvation"* (Psalm 69:13). The phrase *"an acceptable time"* means "a time of pleasure, delight, favor, and goodwill." We are in God's acceptable time. He has invited us to approach Him in faith and confidence. Now is the time for all believers to take their place: the place of prayer. There are people all around us who need to experience the "truth of His salvation," and they are waiting on you and me to pray with all our hearts.

The Power Source of the Prophetic

One day, while I was praying and meditating on the Word of God, the Holy Spirit drew my attention to one of the electrical appliances in my kitchen that was unplugged. He asked me, "Kynan, why won't that appliance turn on?" I answered the Lord, "It is not plugged in!" Then the Lord said to me, "How can you get that appliance to generate power?" My response was simple: "Plug it in!" Then the Lord gave me the most profound message: "Kynan, the reason why many people are not experiencing My power in their lives is because they are not plugged into the power source! Prayer is the power source!"

This was a tremendous revelation for me. I have discovered in my life and ministry that prayer is, in fact, the source of prophetic power for every believer. By prophetic power, I simply mean our ability to manifest God's will and purpose in our lives. Every time we pray in faith, we are tapping into God's supernatural power for our lives. Just as a toaster or a microwave needs to be plugged into a power outlet in order to work, we must stay connected to God—our power Source—through prayer if we want to experience victory and achieve supernatural results.

Again, the Bible tells us in 1 Thessalonians 5:17 to *"pray without ceasing."* Contrary to popular opinion, prayer is not optional. Our Lord commands us to pray! Through prayer, we commune with our heavenly Father. Many years ago, the Lord told me that there were two things that I was not allowed to do: (1) Never come before His people unclean, and (2) never come before His people unprepared. How should one ensure that they are complying with these imperatives? Thankfully, the blood of Jesus Christ washes us clean and enables us to stand before God in righteousness (although we are still required to walk in moral purity). However, the second requirement demands preparation, and preparation can only be achieved when we are intentional about spending time in prayer. A preacher who doesn't pray is like a river without water.

PRAYER IS NOT A LAST RESORT, BUT THE FIRST RESPONSE, FOR EVERY SINCERE BELIEVER.

One day, while in seminary class, my professor shared a very powerful illustration about the necessity of prayer in ministry. There was a pastor who was a very gifted speaker and teacher. One week, the pastor became so busy that he didn't really have time to prayerfully prepare for the message he would deliver the upcoming Sunday. He thought to himself, *I will just minister something from my spirit!* Sunday quickly came, and the pastor was about to go up to the pulpit to preach when the Holy Spirit suddenly arrested him and said, "How dare you assume to speak *for* Me when you haven't spoken *to* Me?" The pastor was so ashamed that he repented in front of the congregation and apologized for having failed to spend time with God before taking the pulpit.

This story stuck with me. It doesn't matter how talented or gifted we are; we must be intentional about spending time in the presence of God. This is the key to developing the spiritual sensitivity we need to follow the leading of the Holy Spirit on a consistent basis. If every believer possesses the spirit of prophecy, then prayer is the spiritual siphon through which we draw on that prophetic power. How many areas of our lives could benefit from God's supernatural solutions? Prayer opens your spiritual self to the supernatural solutions of God. Imagine a life of unlimited access to answers for every problem, situation, or difficulty! Well, guess what? You *already have* unlimited access to divine solutions—through prayer!

Gazing into Eternity

When my wife and I were planting our first church in Tampa, we held prayer meetings every week in our living room. We felt that this was a necessary component to building a strong church. Every Thursday night, my wife and I and a few others would come together and intercede for specific requests as well as pray over the city of Tampa. We prayed for our children, for our church, for our extended family members, and for the challenges we were facing in ministry. The more we prayed, the more evident it became that God was shifting things in our lives. One night as we were praying, the Spirit of God manifested in a very powerful way. The glory of God filled the room. It was in this moment that I felt the unction to make prophetic declarations over our city and ministry. The Spirit of God revealed the heart of the Father to me. I was looking beyond the veil of our natural reality and gazing into eternity.

The Bible says, *"While we look not at the things which are seen, but **at the things which are not seen**: for the things which are seen are temporal; but the things which are not seen are eternal"* (2 Corinthians 4:18). Every time we pray with intentionality, we are accessing the realm of the eternal. In other words, the things that we see in the natural realm are temporal, or subject to time and change, while the things in the spiritual realm are eternal—ageless and everlasting. I often say that the spiritual realm is of a deeper and truer reality than the physical realm. Prayer enables us to connect with the unseen, with that deeper and truer reality. There are eternal realities from the heart of God that He wants to reveal to us on a regular basis, if we would only commune with Him.

PRAYER CHANGES OUR PRIORITIES BECAUSE IT PUTS NATURAL SITUATIONS IN AN ETERNAL CONTEXT.

Imagine you are going to the movie theater to watch a film in 3-D. Before you can enjoy the wonderful dynamics of the movie, you must first put on a pair of special glasses. These glasses allow your eyes to capture things that you would be otherwise unable to perceive. If you have ever tried watching a 3-D movie without 3-D glasses, you know what I'm talking about. Instead of the dynamics meant to excite and entertain, you see only a blurry image!

The same is true in our spiritual lives. Prayer is your pair of "3-D glasses" for the spiritual realm. Without prayer, the circumstances and situations in our lives will be "blurry," lacking clarity and insight, and overwhelming. We will become frustrated from a lack of vision and understanding. However, once we have become empowered and equipped through prayer, we are able to view things from a supernatural vantage point. In the kingdom of God, believing is seeing. Everything about our ability to overcome adversity and walk in the supernatural is contingent upon the way we see things. How do you see things today?

Developing a Heavenly Perspective

I'd like to share one of the most shockingly "real" experiences I have ever had. I was flying home from an overseas ministry trip when the plane encountered severe turbulence. Whenever this happens, I simply close my eyes and pray. But this time, when I closed my eyes, I found myself in heaven. It was the most beautiful place I had ever seen! I don't know whether this was a vision or an out-of-body experience. I thought the plane had crashed and I had gone to meet Jesus, and my first reaction was, *Oh no, I didn't get to say good-bye to my wife.* Just when I was beginning to enjoy the ambience of heaven, I found myself sitting on the plane again. Then I saw the face of Jesus! The next thing I heard were these words: "Tell My people there is more!" Those words resonated within my spirit, so much so that when I got home, I began teaching my congregation how to develop a heavenly perspective.

What do I mean by the term "heavenly perspective"? Well, in the book of Colossians, the apostle Paul wrote the following: *"If ye then be risen with Christ, seek those things which are above, where Christ sitteth on the right hand of God. Set your affection on things above, not on things on the earth. For ye are dead, and your life is hid with Christ in God"* (Colossians 3:1–3). The word for *"affection"* comes from the Greek word *phroneō*, which means "to be of the same mind, i.e. agreed together, cherish the same views." In short, God wants us to share His viewpoint concerning things in the earthly realm. The only way for us to accomplish this is through prayer.

THROUGH PRAYER, WE RECEIVE A HEAVENLY PERSPECTIVE, WHICH ENABLES US TO TRANSCEND NATURAL LIMITATIONS.

The more time we spend in God's presence, the more of His perspective He superimposes on our lives. When we see things the way He sees them, we can act according to His will and nature. If you have ever flown in an airplane, you will readily acknowledge that things look much different from an altitude of 35,000 feet. The world on the ground suddenly seems incredibly small from such an elevated vantage point. The more frequently we enter the place of prophetic prayer, the less significant our problems become, until they assume their actual size: miniature bumps on the grand map of God's plan.

Not only that, but when we *see* from God's perspective, we can *speak* from God's perspective. The Bible says that our citizenship is in heaven. (See Philippians 3:20 NKJV.) Have you ever thought about the deep significance of this biblical truth? Have you ever considered that the circumstances of our lives are nothing compared to the power of God at work within us? Every time we pray, we are declaring that the heavenly realm takes preeminence over the natural realm. I don't know about you, but I want to operate from the heavenly dimension rather than the natural dimension. Our perspective is extremely important. The way we see things will determine our response to them. If we want to respond differently, we must view things differently. We must develop a heavenly perspective so that we can experience heavenly results!

Prophetic Vision

Back when I was trying to get my driver's license, I was required to pass a number of evaluations before I could take my practical driving test. The first was an eye exam. The purpose of the eye exam, of course, was to make sure that I had the ability to see the road and other drivers clearly. Thankfully, I passed both the visual exam and the driving test, and I received my driver's license that day. That eye exam is an apt illustration in our discussion of the life of prayer. If you and I are going to be effective in prophetic prayer, we must first develop prophetic vision. Once our spiritual eyesight becomes 20/20, we will begin to see things from God's perspective.

Remember, in the spiritual realm, we always move toward what we see or discern is the right direction. Spiritual sight and discernment are extremely important, because *"where there is no vision, the people perish: but he that keepeth the law, happy is he"* (Proverbs 29:18). The word for *"vision"* here comes from the Hebrew word *chazown*, or "prophetic vision." What does the Bible mean by "prophetic vision"? Simply put, prophetic vision is the ability to see prophetically, or to see through the lens of God's Word; it is the supernatural ability to peer into the spiritual realm.

When we exercise prophetic vision, we see things clearly, regardless of any chaos that may surround us. But when we lack prophetic vision, we end up accepting things that God never ordained. This is why the Bible says that without vision, *"people perish"* (literally, cast off restraint or let go). The first thing the enemy tries to sabotage in the life of believers is their vision, because he recognizes its power. The enemy knows that if he can cloud your vision, he can ultimately cloud your destiny. The good news is that God is in the business of restoring both spiritual and physical sight.

PROPHETIC VISION GRANTS US THE ABILITY TO TRANSCEND NATURAL CIRCUMSTANCES.

Many years ago, when my wife and I were just starting our ministry, we would go out every weekend and share the gospel with strangers on the street. After one very exhausting and unsuccessful day, we came home distraught and discouraged. I began to complain about the lack of results we were seeing and the negative attitude of our team. In the middle of my rant, my wife stopped me and asked me a question: "Kynan, what do you see?" At first, I didn't understand what she was asking me, so I continued to complain. She asked again, "What do you see?" All of a sudden, I realized that she was not talking about the natural, but the spiritual. Then I began to get the revelation from the Spirit of God that our circumstances were not the truth; rather, the Word of God was the truth.

I closed my eyes and began to see thousands of souls being saved, healed, and delivered. I saw families being restored. I saw the church growing and thriving. Then I began to declare everything I had seen in the Spirit. The next Sunday, we had the largest attendance we had ever seen up to that point. Hallelujah! That's the power of prophetic vision.

The more you meditate on the Word of God, the more you will see things the way He does, and the more you will speak the way He does. Jesus possessed prophetic vision. That is the reason He anticipated events before they came to pass, such as in the following example from John 1:48: *"Nathanael saith unto him, Whence knowest thou me? Jesus answered and said unto him, Before that Philip called thee, when thou wast under the fig tree, I saw thee.*" How was Jesus able to see Nathanael from such a long distance? He was utilizing prophetic vision. When a person exercises prophetic vision, he sees things that others can't see. You and I possess the same prophetic vision as Jesus did, through the Holy Spirit. *Hallelujah!*

Prophetic Prayer

Father, in the name of Jesus, I thank You for who You are and for all that You have done. I declare in the name of Jesus Christ that I have intimacy with the Holy Spirit. I have a personal relationship with You through Your Spirit. I hear the voice of the Holy Spirit on a consistent basis. I am Your sheep, and I hear Your voice, Lord. I will not listen or respond to the voice of a stranger. I can discern the voice of the Lord. I hear from You clearly regarding major decisions in my life. I receive strategic direction from the Holy Spirit as it relates to my finances, relationships, career, calling, witnessing, and every other area in my life. I love to hear the voice of the Spirit. I decree that every voice of authority in my life that is not the voice of the Holy Spirit is silenced right now, in Jesus' name! I thank You, Father, in the name of Jesus, that Your Spirit dwells on the inside of me. Thank You for empowering me to exemplify the life of the Spirit of God to everyone around me. Thank You for the supernatural that flows in and through me. I decree and declare that I am a conduit of divine activity. The world around me is shifted and molded by Your love that operates through me. I have the victory in every area of my life. In Jesus' name, amen!

Prophetic Insights

1. How often should Christians pray?

2. What are the two simultaneous realities in which we live? Which of these realities is greater, or "more true"?

3. What are some difficult circumstances or "pressures" you are experiencing that could be an opportunity for God to birth the prophetic into your life?

PROPHETIC PRACTICUM

1. Study Revelation 19:10, and then ask the Lord to manifest the spirit of prophecy in your everyday life.

2. Make a list of people for whom you are praying, and ask the Lord to give you a word of wisdom concerning those individuals.

3. Ask God to give you a prophetic word for a coworker, classmate, friend, or family member. Pray for discernment of God's timing on when and how to release this word to them (if at all).

4. Commit an hour a day to praying over yourself, your family, and your loved ones. Pray that God will give you a prophetic perspective concerning the circumstances of your life.

3

Beyond the Veil

And, behold, the veil of the temple was rent in twain from the top to the bottom; and the earth did quake, and the rocks rent.
—Matthew 27:51

In the Old Testament, the role of the prophet was an exclusive, sacred office. Only a few people were given the right to prophesy. The same was true of most aspects of worship in the Old Testament, including the priestly office. In fact, the temple system of worship was so strict and particular that those who violated the ordinances faced severe consequences—including death! During the time of Christ, there was a very strict hierarchy in which the religious leaders mediated between the people and their God. The idea of "regular people" experiencing intimate encounters with God would have been considered heretical.

The two dominant religious groups during the time of Christ were the Pharisees and the priests. The Pharisees were strict observers of the law and were responsible for teaching and instructing the people according to its precepts. The priests were responsible for making animal sacrifices and administering the sacraments of the temple. The focal point of both the priests and the Pharisees was the temple.

During the time of Christ, the temple in Jerusalem had two veils: one veil separating the Holy Place from the outer court, and one veil separating the Holy of Holies from the Holy Place. These veils were necessary to prevent unauthorized people from entering the Holy Place and the Holy of Holies. Commoners were restricted to the outer court and could not enter into the Holy Place. But the priests, acting as representatives, were authorized to enter the Holy Place to burn incense, pray, and change the showbread in a ritual that occurred either daily or weekly. The Holy of Holies, on the other hand, was entered just once a year, and then only by the high priest—no one else.

THROUGH CHRIST'S DEATH ON THE CROSS, THE VEIL OF THE TEMPLE HAS BEEN TORN DOWN!

In the book of Matthew, the Bible records that the veil of the temple was rent in two, from top to bottom. (See Matthew 27:51.) This event was very significant and prophetic because it symbolized in a dramatic, tangible way that there was no more need for a high priest to enter the Holy of Holies once a year to offer a sacrifice on behalf of the people. Jesus Christ, the ultimate High Priest, went into the Holy of Holies and sacrificed not the blood of bulls and goats but His own blood on the heavenly altar, once and for all, in fulfillment of Old Testament prophecy.

Through the blood of Jesus, you and I have been granted access to the most sacred place: the Holy of Holies. This means that we no longer have to be relegated to an "outer-court" experience with God! We can draw close to Him in the full assurance of faith that our prayers are being heard and accepted before our almighty God. The veil of separation between God and man has been done away with by the Messiah.

As the author of Hebrews put it,

Having therefore, brethren, boldness to enter into the holiest by the blood of Jesus, by a new and living way, which he hath consecrated for us, through the veil, that is to say, his flesh; and having an high priest over the house of God; let us draw near with a true heart in full assurance of faith, having our hearts sprinkled from an evil conscience, and our bodies washed with pure water.　　　　(Hebrews 10:19–22)

We no longer need to stand "afar off" in worship and prayer. Because of the blood of Jesus, we can draw near to God without any sense of fear, shame, or condemnation.

Priests and Prophets

In the Old Testament, the priest and the prophet were central figures in the worship of God and the observance of His laws. Before the Bible was written, the children of Israel relied on the prophets to receive and transmit the Word of the Lord and on the priests to intercede on their behalf. Under the new covenant established by the shed blood of Jesus, however, you and I have been given both the prophetic and priestly anointing. We no longer need to depend on someone else to hear from God and then relay the message to us. Although the office of prophet is still relevant and necessary, we no longer need to go to a prophet to receive direction; rather, we can hear what the Holy Spirit is saying to us directly, on a daily basis, because we have His anointing: *"But the anointing which ye have received of him abideth in you, and ye need not that any man teach you"* (1 John 2:27).

Under the old covenant, the anointing of the Holy Spirit rested only on certain individuals, externally; but under the new covenant, every believer has access to the prophetic anointing via the Holy Spirit, who lives within. This internal anointing gives us direct access to God's divine direction for our lives. In the Old Testament, not everyone had access to the altar of God—the place of prayer, sacrifice, and intercession; the people had to rely on priests to serve as mediators. God accepted the prayers of the people through the intercession of the priests. However, thanks to Christ's death on the cross, it is no longer necessary for a priest to mediate between God and His children, because Jesus, our High Priest, was the final Mediator. Through Him, we have eternal access to the Father.

And for this cause [Jesus] *is the **mediator** of the new testament, that by means of death, for the redemption of the transgressions that were under the first testament, they which are called might receive the promise of eternal inheritance.* (Hebrews 9:15)

In essence, every believer is a priest and a prophet because of what Jesus did on the cross.

THROUGH THE BLOOD OF JESUS, EVERY BELIEVER HAS RECEIVED THE PRIESTLY MINISTRY OF INTERCESSION.

You may not have viewed yourself as a priest unto God, but that is exactly what you are! As it says in Revelation, "*Jesus Christ...hath made us **kings and priests** unto God and his Father*" (Revelation 1:5–6). The word for "*priests*" here is the Greek word *hiereus*, which means "one who offers sacrifices and in general is busied with sacred rites." In other words, we have been given the same access to God that the priests had in the Old Testament. We can make intercession to God on behalf of others—in particular, on behalf of those who don't have a relationship with Him. We can draw near to God, in spite of our own frailties and limitations.

In the Old Testament, the high priest had to offer sacrifices for himself to atone for his personal sins before he could offer sacrifices to cover the sins of others. His right to function within this office was limited to his ability to perform all the rituals required by the law. The moment the priest failed to fulfill the righteous requirements of the law, he was no longer qualified to operate within that office. For example, if the high priest entered the Holy of Holies wearing a garment with even one blemish, he would be struck dead. (See, for example, Leviticus 21:21.) That sounds pretty scary, doesn't it? Thankfully, under the new covenant, our priestly office is not based on our own righteousness but on the righteousness of Christ. Jesus is our perfect High Priest! (See Hebrews 8:1.)

UNDER THE NEW COVENANT, EVERY BELIEVER HAS BEEN GIVEN THE ABILITY AND THE RIGHT TO MAKE PETITIONS TO THE FATHER IN JESUS' NAME.

The Name of Jesus

One of the most profound truths that I have discovered as a believer is the power and authority of the name of Jesus. Most believers don't realize the significance of the name of Jesus. But hear what Jesus told His disciples: *"And in that day ye shall ask me nothing. Verily, verily, I say unto you, Whatsoever ye shall ask the Father in my name, he will give it you"* (John 16:23). The term *"name"* here is not simply referring to a title; it is the Greek expression *onoma*, which is "used for everything which the name covers, everything the thought or feeling of which is aroused in the mind by mentioning, hearing, remembering, the name, i.e. for one's rank, authority, interests, pleasure, command, excellences, deeds, etc." This is very powerful!

Jesus told His disciples that they no longer needed to come to Him to speak to the Father. Through His name (that is, His personality, character, power, and authority), they could ask the Father directly; and whatever they asked the Father in His name (*onoma*) would be given to them.

This divine reality is amazing! Have you accepted it yet? Whatever we ask the Father in Jesus' name will be given to us! Some people argue that God will not answer every prayer. They suggest that some things are "just not the Father's will." However, the name of Jesus is more than just a filler for us to use as we close out our prayers. To pray in Jesus' name is to pray according to the character and nature of Jesus. The Bible tells us that Jesus is the Word! (See John 1:1–3.) In other words, to pray in Jesus' name is to pray according to the Word of God. Every time we pray according to God's Word, we are guaranteed to receive divine answers.

EVERY TIME WE PRAY IN JESUS' NAME,
WE ARE ALIGNING OURSELVES WITH HEAVEN
AND POSTURING OURSELVES TO RECEIVE
SUPERNATURAL BREAKTHROUGH!

Praying, Not Hoping or Wishing

It is somewhat embarrassing to admit this, but there was a time in my life when I was frustrated with God because my prayers seemed to be falling on deaf ears. I would pray, but it seemed like nothing was changing. There were several times when I confidently told my wife that God was going to come through, and to my surprise nothing happened—at least, that I could see! The more this occurred, the more frustrated I became.

A common topic of my prayers at that time was money. For the first couple of years of our marriage, my wife and I struggled financially. On one memorable occasion, my wife and I got very behind on our car payments, and the bank was threatening to repossess our vehicle. This was no problem for us, since I was a man of supernatural faith! I told my wife that God was going to work it out. I prayed to the Lord, "Please, let us keep the car—in Jesus' name!" but the whole time I was very worried and anxious. I asked several friends if I could borrow some money to catch up on the car payments, and then I sat back to watch God work. Things didn't exactly work out as I had envisioned.

You can probably imagine the look on my face when our vehicle disappeared from the driveway one day. I almost wondered whether the car had been caught up in the rapture. I was very angry! I went to God and demanded to know how He could have allowed something like that to happen. I told Him, "God, I thought You said that if I prayed in faith and asked in Your name, everything would work out!" The Lord responded, "I have nothing to do with this!" Then I asked, "Lord, what do You mean?" The Spirit of the Lord then spoke these words: "Your confidence was never in Me; it was in yourself. To pray in faith is to trust My Word and place your confidence in My power!"

I was praying "in Jesus' name," but not really. And I was not alone—many people do this very thing. To pray in Jesus' name is to stand on the authority of His Word and to rely completely upon Him. Many of us tend to pray about situations and then proceed to "work them out" on our own. But when we try to manipulate the outcome of our circumstances in our own strength and abilities, we fail to approach God with the character and nature of Jesus; we operate in fear instead of faith, and we cannot simultaneously stand on the authority of Jesus' name and be in fear. The nature of Jesus is always faith in God's Word!

I learned a very valuable lesson the day our car disappeared: there is a significant difference between praying in faith and wishing or hoping. I was not in proper alignment with heaven, and, as a result, I was not in a position to receive the breakthrough I desperately desired. Ultimately, God worked everything out, but this lesson was forever burned into my heart.

The Divine Partnership of Prayer

Contrary to popular belief, prayer is not a passive reaction to circumstances in which we wait for God to do something "if it be His will." Prayer is, in fact, a divine partnership between God and man. That's right—we have a part to play in seeing our prayers come to pass. The moment we understand the part we play, the more effective our prayer lives will be, and the sooner we will see supernatural results from God. Earlier, we discussed the importance of praying in Jesus' name. This is the inheritance that we have received as born-again, Spirit-filled believers: the right to use His name. In fact, the more familiar we become with the character and authority of Jesus as we meditate on the Word of God, the more powerful our prayers will become. This revelation on partnering with God in prayer has revolutionized my life.

The Bible says, *"For we are laborers together with God: ye are God's husbandry, ye are God's building"* (1 Corinthians 3:9). The Greek word used for *"laborers together"* is *synergos*, which means "a companion in work." This word is where we get the English term "synergy," defined as the cooperative interaction between two or more substances to produce a combined effect. In other words, God is inviting the believer to cooperate with Him in advancing His kingdom and bringing His will to pass in the earth. We know that God is all-powerful, and we also know that God is relational. As such, He desires our participation and agreement as He moves in the earthly realm.

INTERCESSION IS MORE THAN MERELY PRAYING FOR SOMEONE ELSE; IT IS A DIVINE PARTNERSHIP BETWEEN GOD AND THE BELIEVER THAT RELEASES GOD'S SUPERNATURAL POWER TO BRING CHANGE AND TRANSFORMATION.

I want you think about the biggest problem or the most difficult circumstance you are facing right now. What change do you desire to see? What change does God desire to see? When there is a synergy between what God desires and what you desire, your prayers become an explosive force in the hand of God to bring about supernatural change in your life. Many times, we are waiting on God to do something, and He is waiting on us to pray prophetic prayers as we release our faith, so that He can manifest His purposes in and through us.

Let me tell you about another occasion when I was in desperate need of a financial breakthrough. I kept asking the Lord to bless me financially so that I could do the things He was asking me to do in ministry. Then, one day, I had a revelation! I was reading the Bible, and I came across this verse:

And God is able to make all grace (every favor and earthly blessing)
come to you in abundance, so that you may always and under all cir-
cumstances and whatever the need be self-sufficient [possessing enough
to require no aid or support and furnished in abundance for every good
work and charitable donation]. (2 Corinthians 9:8 AMP)

When I read this Scripture, a lightbulb turned on in my spirit. I said,
"God, Your Word says that it is Your will for me to possess every favor and
earthly blessing so that I can be furnished in abundance for every good
work. Therefore, I command Your supernatural provision to manifest in
my life!" Then I went outside to the mailbox and began to release prophetic
prayers over it. I told my mailbox, "From now on, you are a receptacle of
divine resources!"

I didn't even know what I was doing, but I felt the power of God all
over me. To my amazement, we received thousands of dollars in that very
mailbox within a few days. I want you to understand that this is not about a
religious formula. I'm not telling you to go pray over your mailbox! Rather,
I'm giving you the revelation that we have a responsibility to partner with
God in prayer and to prophesy over every area of our lives. Essentially, I
was praying in Jesus' name! This is the key to seeing supernatural results
to our prayers.

What if I told you that there are no limits to what God can do in your
life through prayer? What if I told you that the key to miracles and breakthrough is a revelation of the power of prophetic prayer?

Open, Sesame!

In the famous Arabic folk tale "Ali Baba and the Forty Thieves," the
expression "Open, sesame" is the password to open the mouth of a cave that
contained priceless treasure. It is believed that the phrase originated from
the ancient Hebrew word *šem*, which means "name" or "name of heaven."
Just as the expression "Open, sesame" was the key to accessing hidden treasure in the folk tale, Jesus is the name that heaven recognizes—the "key"
that gives us unlimited access to the "hidden treasures" of the spiritual
realm.

The name of Jesus is the only legal access key to the spiritual realm. The gospel of John records these words of Jesus: *"I am **the way**, **the truth**, and **the life**: no man cometh unto the Father, but by me"* (John 14:6). The word for *"way"* is the Greek word *hodos*, which means "a travelled way, road." In other words, the name of Jesus is the "way" to supernatural power, provision, breakthrough, and miracles. Unlike the mythical phrases used in folklore, His name is holy, pure, and righteous! We have been given the legal right to use His name, which is the divine access code to the supernatural. No matter what you are facing in your life today, take courage, because you already hold the key to walking in victory. You have His name; now, it is time to *use* it!

Prophetic Prayer

Father, in the name of Jesus, I thank You for who You are and for all that You have done. I declare that my body is the temple of the Holy Spirit, and I am not my own. Your Word commands me in 1 Thessalonians 4 to walk in purity; therefore, I declare that I walk in purity. I possess my body in sanctification and honor. My body is used only for that which is holy and pure. I do not allow contaminants to enter my body, whether they be in the form of intoxicants, foods, movies, images, suggestions, words, or anything else that would defile my body. I accept the truth that my body is sacred, and I yield my body parts as vessels of righteousness. God carries out His mission and purpose through my body, in the name of Jesus Christ. I live to do Your will, oh God! Your commandments are my pleasure to keep. Your commandments are not grievous to me, but I delight myself in Your Word. Today, I look for opportunities to obey Your voice. I am Your obedient child. I think in terms of consistent obedience. My heart is receptive to divine instruction. I will see Your commands through to their completion and fulfillment in my life. Because of my obedience to Your Word, I will see the manifestation of Your promises in my life *today*! In Jesus' name, amen!

Prophetic Insights

1. How are the Old Testament roles of prophet and priest still relevant to the lives of believers today?

2. What is the difference between praying in faith and wishing or hoping?

3. What positive changes can you accomplish by partnering with God through prayer *today*?

4

Approaching the Throne of Grace

*Let us therefore come boldly unto the **throne of grace**, that we may obtain mercy, and find grace to help in time of need.*
—Hebrews 4:16

Earlier, we introduced the concept of God as the righteous Judge. This simply means that God is sovereign over all His creation. The Scriptures also clearly tell us that He is both Lord and King.

In ancient times, kings ruled their kingdoms with power and judgment. It was customary for kings to make the final decisions in legal matters, land disputes, and all religious, social, and economic situations—all while seated on their throne, which represented their power, royalty, and government.

During biblical times, the idea of approaching a king's throne was very dreadful because it was a matter of life and death. Think of the incredible scene in the book of Esther when Esther courageously decides to enter the throne room without being summoned. Unless the king offered mercy, the default was execution! (See Esther 4:10–16.) There was no turning back. One mistake, and she would have been sentenced to death.

The author of Hebrews, in Hebrews 4:16, makes an interesting allusion to God's throne, as well as the mercy seat in the Old Testament tabernacle: *"Let us therefore come boldly unto the throne of grace, that we may obtain mercy, and find grace to help in time of need."* What is a "mercy seat," and what does it have to do with prayer? The mercy seat was one of the most significant items in the old covenant because it was the lid to the ark of the covenant, which housed the divine testimony of God. (See, for example, Exodus 26:34.) This seat carried the manifest presence of God. A symbolic replica of His throne, it represented His royal power and holiness. The irony of its being called the "mercy seat" is that people died just from touching it. Why? Because God is so holy that He cannot coexist with sin—hence the definition of *holy*: "separate from sin." When anyone touched the mercy seat in the Old Testament, it was deadly, because the presence of a holy God was incompatible with sinful man. All men—including the high priest himself—were at the "mercy" of God's law.

WE NO LONGER NEED TO APPROACH GOD IN FEAR OR DREAD, BECAUSE WE HAVE BEEN MADE ACCEPTABLE TO HIM THROUGH THE BLOOD OF JESUS.

However, notice that the author of Hebrews does not refer to it as the mercy seat anymore, but as the *"throne of grace."* What changed? Under the old covenant, men attempted to approach God to find mercy, but they were incapable of keeping His commands and were thereby prevented from receiving the very mercy they were seeking. Under the new covenant, however, we no longer approach the "mercy seat," which was a throne of judgment. Instead, we approach the throne of God's grace, which enables and empowers us to overcome every sin and weakness. This is possible because Jesus, acting on our behalf, entered into the heavenly Holy of Holies and placed

His blood upon the mercy seat. He forever changed the mercy seat from a throne of judgment to a *"throne of grace"* for everyone who believes in Him.

Sin Consciousness

For many years, I operated under the misguided belief that God was always angry with me. Whenever I would fail in my relationship with God, I would consider myself unworthy to pray to Him or to be in His presence. I was dealing with an Old Testament "mercy seat" mentality. I did not even realize I possessed it until God revealed it to me. Because of this mentality, I was never really sure if my prayers were being heard, let alone if they would be answered. Just as a pauper is at the mercy of his or her king, in my mind, I was at the mercy of a judgmental God who would arbitrarily deal out either kindness or wrath. This misinformed mind-set was an unfortunate consequence of focusing on my own sin instead of on God's grace.

You may be in the same place I was in years ago. You may still believe that you are sinful and unworthy. You may view God as a harsh, fickle, and demanding king. Ultimately, we are at the mercy of God; after all, He is sovereign, and we are not! However, He has made loving promises to us that we must claim. If we don't believe that we are acceptable to Him, then we will never approach Him with boldness and confidence. Instead, we will be manipulated by a fear that keeps us from God's presence.

Again, the author of Hebrews tells us to come boldly in order to receive mercy. When the Bible uses the expression *"obtain mercy"* (Hebrews 4:16), it is using the Greek word *lambanō*, which means "to take with the hand, lay hold of,...to take to oneself." The idea is that of laying claim to something with a sense of entitlement or ownership. In the Old Testament, the priest walked into the Holy of Holies with a sense of fear and uncertainty, because one violation of the law could cost him his life. I am reminded of Uzzah the Levite, who attempted to catch the ark of the covenant as it began to fall during transport. Because he violated the commandment that forbade touching the ark, he died instantly. (See 2 Samuel 6:1–7.)

Now, however, you and I have been invited to "lay hold of" the grace of God and to receive divine pardon for our failures and empowerment (grace) for our every area of need. The same thing that caused death under the old covenant now gives life under the new covenant.

The enemy knows the supernatural power of prayer, and the last thing he wants is for us to walk boldly into our prayer closets. To stop us from being effective in prayer, he attempts to constantly remind us of our sins and failures. This is what I meant earlier by the term "sin consciousness," or the tendency of believers to be more aware of their own sin than of God's righteousness. Under this dispensation of grace, it seems that the need for personal responsibility and moral purity has been lost in translation. I am not negating our responsibility to walk in holiness, but I am suggesting that too many believers have allowed their lives to be controlled by guilt, shame, and condemnation. God doesn't want us to be obsessed with our failures, or any other aspect of ourselves. He wants us to be free to worship Him in spirit and in truth. (See John 4:23.)

THROUGH THE BLOOD OF JESUS CHRIST, GOD HAS USHERED IN A NEW AND ETERNAL PRIESTHOOD FOR EVERY BELIEVER.

The *truth* is that there are issues God needs us to address in prayer. He deeply desires to commune with us on a regular basis, but He cannot do that if we are walking around in bondage and despair. I believe that there are heavenly "downloads" that God wants to deposit into our inner being every day. These downloads consist of solutions, inventions, strategies, and divine wisdom for life's challenges, as well as empowerment and refreshment. To receive these downloads, however, we must learn to approach the throne of grace daily.

If you are battling sinful behaviors and habits that you feel would somehow disqualify you from receiving God's grace, I have great news for you. The Bible says, *"If we confess our sins, he is faithful and just to forgive us our sins, and to cleanse us from all unrighteousness"* (1 John 1:9). Simply acknowledge your wrongdoing with a repentant heart, turn away from it, and thank God for the blood of Jesus that cleanses you of all sin.

EVERY TIME WE ACKNOWLEDGE OUR FAILURES
WITH HUMILITY AND GRACE, WE DISEMPOWER
THE VOICE OF THE ACCUSER.

The Full Assurance of Faith

There is no denying that faith is a key component to receiving answers to prayer. The Bible tells us that without faith, it is impossible to please God; he that comes to God must believe that He is, and that He rewards those who seek Him. (See Hebrews 11:6.) Every time we come to God, we must come to Him in faith. As you may know by now, the word *faith* means conviction, confidence, and trust. The writer of Hebrews says, *"Let us draw near with a true heart in **full assurance of faith**, having our hearts sprinkled from an evil conscience, and our bodies washed with pure water"* (Hebrews 10:22). What is meant by *"full assurance of faith"*? The term *"full assurance"* comes from the Greek word *plērophoria*, which means "most certain confidence."

Many years ago, I was in the insurance business. Even though I sold *insurance*, the real commodity I sold was *assurance*. The dictionary defines *assurance* as a positive declaration intended to give confidence; a promise. By furnishing people with health insurance, I was providing them with the assurance that they would be covered financially in case of a medical emergency. What assurance do we have in prayer? Jesus said, *"What things soever ye desire, when ye pray, believe that ye receive them, and **ye shall have them**"* (Mark 11:24).

When we come to God, we must release our faith in His power and promises for our lives. This is why a knowledge of our right standing with God is of supreme importance in prayer. Without confidence in His Word, we can't boldly claim His promises. The devil knows that if he can erode our confidence in God, he can undermine our faith walk, and ultimately keep us from receiving answers to our prayers. Give him no place!

I believe a revelation of divine faith is the key to seeing the miraculous manifest through prayer. I want to encourage you with the news that you are qualified to approach God in prayer, not based on your own merit but based on His unmerited favor and goodness. This news should fill you with confidence that will enable you to transcend every natural limitation you face. You will begin to see the supernatural manifest in your life like never before. In our ministry in Tampa, we are seeing thousands of people activated in the power of God through prayer. Many of them never thought they were "spiritual enough" or "qualified" to pray for others, but now they realize that their ability to receive answers to prayer is not based on their own goodness or righteousness but on their faith in God's unlimited power.

WE ARE CLOAKED IN ROBES OF RIGHTEOUSNESS; THEREFORE, WE BELONG IN GOD'S PRESENCE.

The Bible says, "*Therefore it is of faith, that it might be by grace; to the end the promise might be sure to all the seed; not to that only which is of the law, but to that also which is of the faith of Abraham; who is the father of us all*" (Romans 4:16). Faith activates the supernatural grace of God in our lives. Whether we are praying for the healing of a loved one, pleading for the salvation of our spouse, or making any other heartfelt request, the key is tapping into the grace of God by faith. Remember, the grace of God is not simply unmerited favor; it is also the divine power of God made available to accomplish what we cannot. A revelation that we are completely loved and accepted by the Father is the catalyst for boldness in prayer.

A Testimony of Prophetic Prayer

In our church in Tampa, we often have new believers join our church with no understanding of spiritual things. These individuals are often very perplexed by the realm of the supernatural and the idea that they can hear God's voice. Many of them feel that they do not qualify, or that they are not "religious" or knowledgeable enough to confidently walk in the miraculous. After all, they have been saved for just a short period of time; they have not had an opportunity to gain as much Bible knowledge as the pastors and other leaders of the church.

However, as these believers learn the Word and begin to gain a proper understanding of their identity in Christ as beloved, righteous priests unto God, they receive the boldness to pray—and they see results! One such young lady, who had just joined the church and been recently baptized, approached my wife and me and asked, "How do you hear God's voice? I know I should be hearing it, but I just don't know how. And I don't understand how to walk in the supernatural that you are always talking about. What am I missing?"

What she was missing was an understanding of who she was in Christ. The more she gained the revelation of her rights to approach the throne of grace, the more her boldness grew. And the more confident she became, the more she prayed and sought the Lord. She came to understand that she had as much of a right as anyone else to be heard by God and to hear from God. As she grew in faith and became more assured of her position in God's eyes, her spiritual eyes were opened. First, she received some vivid revelatory dreams from the Lord. Next, she began to see in the Spirit, with God showing her specific things about certain people. After that, she started hearing God's audible voice speaking to her, and she would prophesy with boldness, knowing she had heard from God. And every time this happened, God would confirm that the things she had spoken were indeed from Him. She even began to lay hands on sick people and see the instant healing of those she prayed for, including her spiritual leaders.

This young woman was not a special case at our church. Countless young people coming to our church began to experience the same things. Even those who had not been attending our church for very long started hearing accurately from God, then prophesying, releasing words of wisdom and words of knowledge, praying, and seeing miracles manifest in response to their prayers. This incredible, supernatural lifestyle was activated when these individuals received a revelation of who God said they were.

Lessons from a Canaanite Woman

The gospel of Matthew includes a very powerful illustration of the grace and power of God in action. In Matthew 15, Jesus encounters a Canaanite woman who is in desperate need of a miracle.

> *And, behold, a woman of Canaan came out of the same coasts, and cried unto him, saying, Have mercy on me, O Lord, thou Son of David; my daughter is grievously vexed with a devil.* (Matthew 15:22)

Jesus' initial response to this woman was quite shocking: He ignored her request. Can you imagine how that woman must have felt? Probably discouraged and dejected, to say the least. When Jesus' disciples asked Him to deal with the crying woman, Jesus told them, *"I am not sent but unto the lost sheep of the house of Israel"* (Matthew 15:24). In other words, Jesus was saying that this woman did not meet the religious requirements for receiving a miracle. She was not qualified because she was not a Jew!

Not only that, but as a Canaanite, she was looked down upon by the Jewish community as an idolater. That this woman would approach Jesus in a public setting was culturally unacceptable and downright laughable. However, this woman was not willing to give up on her miracle that easily. The Bible says that she *"came and worshipped [Jesus], saying, Lord, help me"* (Matthew 15:25).

The type of worship this woman was doing was not the same as our modern concept of worship. In ancient times, to worship meant to bow to the ground and make obeisance in an act of reverential acknowledgement. There were two primary categories of people at this time who would have received this kind of worship: kings and priests. By bowing at the feet of our Lord, the Canaanite woman was acknowledging Jesus' kingly and priestly authority.

To add insult to injury, Jesus responded to her worship with these words: *"It is not meet to take the children's bread, and to cast it to dogs"* (Matthew 15:26). I often joke that most of us would have canceled our membership in Jesus' church at this point. Yet the response of this woman was extremely unorthodox, and full of belief:

And she said, Truth, Lord: yet the dogs eat of the crumbs which fall from their masters' table. Then Jesus answered and said unto her, **O woman, great is thy faith**: *be it unto thee even as thou wilt. And her daughter was made whole from that very hour.* (Matthew 15:27–28)

This is an amazing testimony! Why was Jesus so moved by this woman's words, and why did He consider them as such a great display of faith? Simply put, the Canaanite woman received a revelation that the miracle she so desperately desired was not going to come based on her own righteousness or ethnic identity, but solely on the goodness, righteousness, and power of Jesus. Each of us must have a "Yes, Lord, but even the dogs..." moment! Like this Canaanite woman, we must approach God's throne knowing that He alone is able. Once we do this, miracles will become our new normal!

Prophetic Prayer

Father, in the name of Jesus, I thank You for who You are and for all You have done in my life. I declare that today is the day of the Lord's favor. I walk in the favor of God today. I acknowledge that through the blood of Christ, I can boldly approach the throne of grace. I acknowledge that although I often fail, You have graciously cloaked me with robes of righteousness. I am distinct from the people around me. I walk in grace and preferential treatment. Doors are supernaturally opened unto me today. I am a magnet of divine favor and supernatural blessings. Everywhere I go today, God will use someone to do something extraordinary for me. The doors of promotion and increase are opened to me today. I will receive both natural and spiritual gifts today. Men shall give into my bosom today. All grace abounds toward me in a way that causes me to have all sufficiency in all areas of my life. I will meet someone today who will favor me financially. People are compelled to do wonderful things for me today. In Jesus' name, amen!

Prophetic Insights

1. How did the "mercy seat" of the Old Testament turn into the "throne of grace" of the New Testament, and what does that transformation mean for believers today?

2. What are the qualifications of a believer to hear the Lord's voice and to walk in the miraculous?

3. Have you ever had a "Yes, Lord, but even the dogs..." moment, as the Canaanite woman did in Matthew 15?

PROPHETIC PRACTICUM

1. Do you believe, deep within, that you are worthy to come before God in prayer? If not, pray through Psalm 51, which is a prayer of repentance, and then read Hebrews 4:16 and ask God for the confidence to *"come boldly unto the throne of grace"* because of what Christ did for you on the cross.

2. Write down a prayer of supplication. Then, go back over the prayer and insert "in Jesus' name" where appropriate, remembering that to pray in Jesus' name means to pray according to the character and nature of Jesus. Does your prayer hold up under that definition? If so, be confident! You are guaranteed to receive divine answers.

3. Review the prayer of supplication you just wrote. Are any of your requests merely *hopes* or *wishes* instead of *prayers of faith*? Ask God to show you how to align yourself with heaven by faith instead of just "crossing your fingers."

5

Understanding Your
Prophetic DNA

*God, who at sundry times and in divers manners spake
in time past unto the fathers by the prophets, hath in these last days
spoken unto us by his Son, whom he hath appointed heir of all things,
by whom also he made the worlds.*
—Hebrews 1:1–2

We have discussed the importance of prayer in great detail. We have discovered that prayer is more than a religious ritual; it is also a powerful means of communion with God. Not only have we examined prayer in general, but we have also endeavored to uncover the prophetic nature of prayer. Again, by "prophetic prayer," we refer to praying in such a way that releases God's will and purposes into the world around us.

Now let me take it a step further: I believe that every child of God is capable of prophesying from God's throne of grace into the various affairs of his or her life!

How is that possible? Well, let me give you an analogy that should help. In the late 1800s, Swiss scientists stumbled upon a very peculiar substance in the pus of discarded surgical bandages. This substance, made up of sugar, phosphate, and nucleic acid, was later determined to be what we now know as deoxyribonucleic acid—more commonly, DNA. Essentially, DNA is a molecule that carries the genetic instructions used in the development and function of all known living organisms. More simply put, DNA determines the characteristics and functionality of every creature.

Just as every human being has a physical DNA that determines his or her physical traits and functions, every believer has a spiritual DNA that determines his or her spiritual function. The Bible says, *"Being **born again**, not of corruptible seed, but of incorruptible, by the word of God, which liveth and abideth for ever"* (1 Peter 1:23). Jesus explained in the Gospels that we must be *"born again"* in order to enter the kingdom of God. (See, for example, John 3:3.) What does the expression "born again" really mean? The word for *"born"* in John 3:3 is the Greek word *gennaō*, which means "to be born, begotten, or engendered." It is from this term that we get the English word "gene." The moment we were born again (that is, came to faith in Jesus), we became carriers of God's genetic code. His DNA lives inside us!

TO BE BORN OF GOD MEANS TO TAKE ON THE NATURE, FUNCTION, AND CHARACTER OF JESUS!

The book of Hebrews opens with this explanation: *"God, who...spoke in time past...by the prophets, has in these last days spoken to us by His Son"* (Hebrews 1:1–2 NKJV). This means that Christ was the last oracle through whom God revealed the mystery of His will. In Christ, we have received the full, complete counsel of God's Word. Jesus is the Word of God personified. If Jesus lives in us by the Holy Spirit, it means that the prophetic Word of God dwells within us. I want you to take a moment and think about the implications of that last statement.

The Scriptures declare, *"Therefore if any man be in Christ, he is a new creature: old things are passed away; behold, all things are become new"* (2 Corinthians 5:17). Through Jesus, God brought into being a creature that had never existed before. The Greek term for this creature is *kaino-ktisis*, "of a new kind, unprecedented,…unheard of." Those of us who have been born of Jesus have become new creations with a supernatural nature. We have received the prophetic nature of Jesus inside our very being. Because of this prophetic nature, we have the capacity and ability to call things into being. Later on in this book, we will talk about the importance of prophetic decrees. For now, I just want to emphasize the amazing nature that we have received. Every time we speak or pray from this divine nature within us, we are indeed speaking and praying prophetically!

You Were Born to Prophesy

Remember, you don't need a special title or an elevated position in the church in order to prophesy. You can release prophecy in your home prayer closet. The moment you gave your life to Christ, you were made a partaker of the same Spirit that raised Jesus from the dead. In that moment, you were born to prophesy!

There was a time when my wife and I were experiencing severe stagnation, both spiritual and physical, in our personal lives and in our ministry. I should have recognized it was a spiritual attack; however, at this point, I lacked an awareness of the demonic spiritual forces at work around us. One day, my wife asked me if we could pray together. Honestly, I was so annoyed by the trial we were enduring that I didn't even have a desire to pray. This fact in itself is a sign that we were under severe spiritual oppression. Reluctantly, I consented to pray. As my wife and I were coming into agreement through prayer, she had a vision in the spiritual realm of a spider web hovering over our house. Caught in that web were all the things we were believing God for, including cars, finances, and other resources.

When my wife divulged her vision to me, I began to prophesy over the situation and commanded the enemy to loosen his stranglehold on our blessings. There was an immediate release in the spiritual realm. Shortly after this, everything my wife had seen in that spider web began to materialize in our lives. Hallelujah! What would have happened if my wife and I had continued to go on without addressing the spiritual opposition that was afflicting us? What would the outcome have been if we had kept "waiting on God" to do something rather than prophesied over our problems? The Hebrew word for *prophesy* is *naba'* (*na-va*), which means "to bring forth under the influence of divine spirit." It literally means to speak with divine emotion. When was the last time you thought of prophecy this way?

AS BELIEVERS, WE DO NOT LIVE IN A FIXED, UNCHANGEABLE REALITY. IF WE CAN SEE IT, THEN WE CAN CHANGE IT—THROUGH PROPHETIC PRAYER!

We have been given the ability to pray with divine emotion. Rather than praying passively, we can tap into God's "emotions" concerning any situation in our lives. Every time we pray, we are drawing from a prophetic river inside our very being. The Bible says, *"He that believeth on me, as the scripture hath said, out of his belly shall flow **rivers of living water**"* (John 7:38). The Greek word used here for *"rivers"* is *potamos*, which means "a river, a torrent, flood." In other words, there is a supernatural torrent on the inside of us that has the power to overtake any and every area of our lives with the presence of God.

Notice that the verse in John says that we have a river within, rather than a well. A river flows continuously from its source, also called the head. Jesus is the Head of the river inside us, and He the Source of limitless prophetic power for every believer. The more conscious we become of His presence in us, the more freely this prophetic torrent will flow in and through us. I don't know about you, but that makes me very excited!

The Office Versus the Nature

It is important to make a distinction between the *office* of prophet and the prophetic *nature*. The Bible tells us in 1 Corinthians, *"And God hath set some in the church, first apostles, secondarily **prophets**, thirdly teachers, after that miracles, then gifts of healings, helps, governments, diversities of tongues"* (1 Corinthians 12:28). This Scripture makes a specific reference to the office of prophet. According to *Strong's Dictionary*, a prophet is "one who, moved by the Spirit of God and hence his organ or spokesman, solemnly declares to men what he has received by inspiration, especially concerning future events, and in particular such as relate to the cause and kingdom of God and to human salvation."

Not everyone is called to the office of the prophet, but only those who have been given the temperament to function in such a capacity. However, every believer has a prophetic nature, as a result of the Spirit of God (who is divine inspiration personified) dwelling within. This means that all believers have been called to pray, minister, and see things from a prophetic perspective. We should not accept things the way they appear in the natural, because we know that there is more than meets the eye. In fact, every time we approach God, whether for own needs or on the behalf of others, we are operating out of our prophetic nature.

Looking into the Heart of Jesus

I want to tell you about a very powerful encounter I had with the Lord. I had been praying for a supernatural experience with Jesus for quite some time. One night, while I was sleeping, the Lord Jesus walked into my room. When I heard Him call my name, I awoke from my sleep. (That was a miracle in itself!) Whether this was a vision or an out-of-body experience, I couldn't tell. The atmosphere of my room was transformed, so that I felt I was experiencing heaven on earth. Jesus stared at me with a soul-piercing gaze. I felt as naked before Him as Adam and Eve had been in the garden of Eden. He didn't have to speak to me audibly, because I knew by the Spirit of God what He was saying. I was almost able to read His mind! It is very hard to articulate this phenomenon.

While I stood there in utter amazement, Jesus did the unimaginable. He reached into His gown and pulled out His heart, and then He extended it toward me. (This was not a gruesome act, by any means.) As I looked into His heart, I saw the nations of the earth. In His heart was every ethnic group, tribe, and tongue. The longer I gazed into His heart, the more I was overcome with emotion. I even began to weep! I knew that His heart was broken over the condition of society. He was hurt by the pain and despair that people were feeling. Even more, He was broken over the misperceptions that people had of Him. He said to me, "People believe that I am the one causing them pain, when, in fact, I died for them to be set free! I am their Healer."

After this experience, I was undone! It left me marveling at how few believers actually know what is on God's heart. Can you imagine being able to tap into the heart of God on a consistent basis? Once we know what is on His heart, we can pray confidently and boldly. You may not have had an encounter like the one I just described, but every time you meditate on the Word of God, you are looking into God's heart.

GOD HAS INVITED US TO GAZE INTO HIS HEART AND SEE HIS DESIRES FOR HIS PEOPLE.

A few years ago, I began to pray this prayer: "Lord, allow me to look into Your heart and see the needs of Your people." Contrary to popular belief, God is concerned about every aspect of our lives. He cares about your health, your children, your finances, and even the type of car you drive. By praying prophetically, we invite Him to invade all the various areas of our lives.

When I was a young believer, I would spend hours in prayer every morning before school. On most occasions, I wouldn't ask God for any particular blessings; I would simply allow Him to impart downloads to my spiritual man. He would show me certain details about people and situations, and then I would pray specifically for those people and situations.

One day while I was in prayer, I had a vision in which a woman and I were praying on opposite sides of a bed. Somehow, I could tell that our location was Africa. The woman had long hair, but I couldn't see her face. I began to pray for that woman, little knowing I was praying for my future wife, Gloria. God has a very interesting sense of humor! Today, my wife labors with me in the international ministry the Lord has given both of us. Together, we have seen many miracles birthed out of prophetic prayer. What does God want to reveal to you today through prayer?

Supernatural Insight

A member of our church shared the following powerful testimony about prayer. She was praying in her room one day when the Lord gave her an impression of a particular person she had never met. As she prayed, the Lord described this person in detail. This woman then received an unction from God to go and minister in a nearby community. She asked her husband if it was ok, then proceeded to go out to the streets. While riding her bike in the community, she encountered the very person she had seen in her prayer. The Lord gave her a word for this person that was a true blessing. Hallelujah!

This woman was not ordained as a minister, nor did she hold a special office in the church. And her experience was not unique among the members of our congregation. Many people in our ministry experience similar events on a regular basis.

The Bible says,

> But as it is written, Eye hath not seen, nor ear heard, neither have entered into the heart of man, the things which God hath prepared for them that love him. But God hath revealed them unto us by his Spirit: for the Spirit searcheth all things, yea, the deep things of God.
>
> (1 Corinthians 2:9–10)

The Holy Spirit is ready and willing to give us divine insight in prayer every day. How many areas of our lives could benefit from these divine solutions? I have often heard people misinterpret 1 Corinthians 2:9, saying that the implication of *"Eye hath not seen..."* is that God's will is somehow a mystery. However, they fail to notice the rest of the verse: *"But God has revealed them to us by his Spirit."* God wants to reveal mysteries to us by the Holy Spirit. He wants to use prayer to show us the things that are to come.

The verse also says that the Spirit *"searcheth all things."* What does this mean, and how is it relevant to prayer? The word for *"searcheth"* is the Greek word *eraunaō*, which means "to examine." In other words, the Spirit of God examines the mind and heart of God, then imparts wisdom, revelation, and insight to the believer. What a marvelous God we serve!

WHEN WE MAKE INTERCESSION UNDER THE INSPIRATION OF THE HOLY SPIRIT, WE ARE LITERALLY INVITING HEAVEN TO INVADE THE EARTH.

In my book *The Power of Unlimited Faith*, I talk about the reality of a life of miracles for every single believer. We can operate in the supernatural dimension every day. How? By communing with the Holy Spirit as often as possible. When we pray intentionally and consistently, we tap into the miraculous power of God. If believers really knew the profound power of prayer, they would make praying a daily priority. If we really understood how prayer can reshape our destinies, the prayer services in our churches would draw crowds to fill the sanctuary. We must become sensitive to what God is speaking to us in prayer!

One day, my wife and I were praying about our church. We were seeking God's instruction on how to go about growing our ministry. Of course, we knew that Jesus is the One who builds the church, and that we are simply His vessels. We also knew that the key to all spiritual growth is obeying the Word of God, and that prayer is part of this obedience. As we were praying, the Lord gave us a specific instruction. He told us to go to a certain area of our city and evangelize there. We obeyed the prompting of the Holy Spirit. The following Sunday, we didn't have enough room to accommodate all the first-time visitors at our church. What happened? We followed the leading of the Holy Spirit, and He gave us insight that led to the exponential growth of our ministry. Hallelujah! As the Bible declares, *"For as many as are **led by the Spirit** of God, they are the sons of God"* (Romans 8:14).

You Have the Mind of Christ

Earlier, we talked about the prophetic nature within each believer. We must learn to tap into this prophetic nature if we want to see God's miraculous power demonstrated in our lives. I don't know about you, but I don't accept the limitations and barriers that the enemy attempts to place upon my life.

The Bible paints a very different picture from the portrait of powerless religion that is often displayed in our modern culture. I believe that we have the grace and ability to transcend the cultural norms of sin, fear, defeat, and brokenness. The Bible says, *"For who hath known the mind of the Lord, that he may instruct him? but we have the **mind of Christ**"* (1 Corinthians 2:16). The Greek word for *"mind"* is *nous*, "the faculties of perceiving and understanding, and those of feeling, judging, determining." We possess the same capacity as Christ to understand, feel, and judge under divine inspiration. We have the mind of Christ! This is a profound truth.

Remember, Jesus walked in perfect communion with the Father every day of His earthly ministry. It is important to realize that the ministry of Jesus was fulfilled not in His deity but in His humanity, saturated by the Holy Spirit. The same Holy Spirit that He possessed (and still possesses) is the same Spirit we possess!

There is an old saying, "Perception is reality." In other words, the way you think—including how you reason and perceive—shapes what you believe to be your reality. This is why it is so important that we renew our mind with the Word of God. (See Romans 12:2.) By meditating continually on God's Word, we develop the mind of Christ and embrace a heavenly perspective. Remember, we are not "going to get" the mind of Christ; we already have it! It's within us!

Right now, I want you to imagine how your prayer life might change when you acknowledge that you have the mind of Christ. Jesus never prayed a single prayer that wasn't answered! He never doubted that His Father heard and accepted Him. In fact, Jesus said to His Father in John 11:42, *"And I knew that thou hearest me always."* The mind of Christ is a mentality of victory.

WHEN YOU ACCEPT THE TRUTH THAT THE MIND OF CHRIST IS WITHIN YOU, YOU WILL PRAY WITH VERACITY AND BOLDNESS.

Learning to think differently causes us to pray differently; and when we begin to pray differently, we see different results. There should be no more asking God to do something "if it be Thy will"! Rather, we should thank the Father in advance, by faith, with confidence that He hears us. We are what we think, according to the Bible: *"For as* [a man] *thinketh in his heart, so is he"* (Proverbs 23:7).

Many people in the body of Christ pray from a victim mentality. I call these people "crisis Christians." These individuals have a tendency to be ruled by the circumstances of their lives, and this tendency extends to their prayer lives. When their circumstances seem calm and peaceful, their prayer lives are pleasant, but when a storm or other type of test arises, they become frantic.

I know about crisis Christians because I used to be one. Crisis Christians remind me of the disciples in the boat with Jesus on the Sea of Galilee when a tumultuous storm sprang up:

> *And there arose a great storm of wind, and the waves beat into the ship, so that it was now full. And [Jesus] was in the hinder part of the ship, asleep on a pillow: and they awake him, and say unto him, Master, carest thou not that we perish? And he arose, and rebuked the wind, and*

said unto the sea, Peace, be still. And the wind ceased, and there was a
great calm. (Mark 4:37–39)

What did Jesus know that the disciples did not? He knew that God was all-powerful and therefore had dominion over the storm. This understanding affected the way Jesus responded to the wind and the waves. Instead of asking God why this was happening to them, He simply said, "*Peace, be still*" (literally, "Sea, be quiet!"). Jesus knew that nothing had the right or the permission to disturb His perfect communion with the Father. It should be no different for you and me! We need to tell every storm of sickness, disease, poverty, and anxiety to be silenced, in Jesus' name. When the issues of life threaten to overwhelm you, simply release a prayer into the atmosphere that will override the tempest of the enemy.

The Spirit of Intercession

Throughout this book, we have examined the power, purpose, and necessity of prophetic prayer. Right now, I want to explore a specific type of prayer: intercession. What is intercession? Why is it significant? The Bible says, "*Wherefore [Jesus] is able also to save them to the uttermost that come unto God by him, seeing he ever liveth to make **intercession** for them*" (Hebrews 7:25). The word "*intercession*" here comes from the Greek word *entygchanō*, which means "to light upon a person, fall in with...to go to or meet a person, especially for the purpose of conversation." This term is very complex, but it essentially implies a meeting or a conversation with God on behalf of someone else (or multiple people). It may involve bearing a burden for others or to *fall in* with someone.

Intercession is a legal term that refers to the mediation or intervention of one party in the dispute of another, with the intent to resolve the conflict. Jesus is our divine Intercessor! He stands before the Father night and day, praying for us. (See Hebrews 7:25.) In the same way, we have received the spirit of intercession. We have the power and responsibility, as Christ's ambassadors in the earthly realm, to intervene through prayer on behalf of others. This is not the same as seeking to control the lives of others; rather, it is passionately praying for others by the leading and inspiration of the

Holy Spirit. When was the last time you really took up someone else's problem or trial in prayer, earnestly imploring the Lord on behalf of that person?

People have a tendency to be self-absorbed and consumed with concern for their own struggles and difficulties. If we succumb to the temptation to focus only on ourselves, we run the risk of missing out on one of the most important ministries of the New Testament: the ministry of intercession. There have been countless times when I was praying for someone and began to weep because I was overwhelmed by God's heart for that person. Unfortunately, many people have been taught to doubt the effectiveness of prayer; therefore, they neglect to take up the mantle of intercession. Let us not be counted among them!

THE SPIRIT OF INTERCESSION OPENS OUR EYES TO DETAILS WE WOULD OTHERWISE MISS.

The Bible commands us to "[pray] *always with all prayer and supplication in the Spirit, and watching thereunto with all perseverance and supplication for all saints*" (Ephesians 6:18). Every time we enter into earnest prayer on the behalf of someone else, we are fulfilling our prophetic mandate outlined in Ephesians 6:18. The ministry of intercession is what we at our church call the "ministry of the interior." God always reveals special details to His intercessors. Keep in mind that God does not support gossip or talebearing; therefore, if He reveals something to us, it is for the purpose of prayer and intercession.

On a trip to England, I had a chance to ride on the London Eye—the huge Ferris wheel overlooking the entire city of London. As our capsule ascended higher and higher, my vantage point expanded, giving me an increasingly better view of the city. This is exactly the way intercession works. The more we intercede, the higher we "ascend," gaining a clearer and clearer view of the spiritual realm. This is why the Bible says, "...*watching thereunto with all perseverance and supplication for all saints."* We are to be spiritual "watchmen," always anticipating the manifestation of God's promises in our lives and in the lives of others. Traditionally, watchmen stood upon the wall in order to gain a superior vantage point of their enemy. God wants to give you and me a superior vantage point over the enemy. And the only way to see things that others can't is by wholeheartedly embracing the ministry of intercession.

Foretelling Versus Forth-Telling

There are two critical aspects of prophecy that are important for every believer to understand: foretelling and forth-telling. But first, let me point out that there is widespread misunderstanding within the body of Christ about the prophetic ministry. Contrary to popular belief, the prophet is not a soothsayer or a psychic. If we are going to be effective in prophetic prayer, we must embrace the true nature of prophecy. The ministry of prophecy was never intended to be a spectacle for people's entertainment.

PROPHECY IS MORE THAN THE FORETELLING OF THE FUTURE; IT IS ALSO THE CALLING FORTH OF THE WILL OF GOD INTO MANIFESTATION.

Foretelling

Foretelling is the prophetic ability to see the future because the Spirit of God has revealed it. Knowledge of this kind is usually expressed as a word of wisdom or a word of knowledge, the latter term typically applying to past or current events rather than future happenings. Another word for this knowledge is *prediction*. The prophets of the Old Testament would receive divine insight into future events and then warn God's people accordingly. This is a very important aspect of prophecy, because the Bible says, *"Surely the Lord God will do nothing without revealing His secret to His servants the prophets"* (Amos 3:7 AMP).

There are also many examples of foretelling in the New Testament. The primary example is our Lord Himself. Jesus foretold the destruction of the temple in Jerusalem: *"And Jesus said unto them, See ye not all these things? verily I say unto you, There shall not be left here one stone upon another, that shall not be thrown down"* (Matthew 24:2). This portion of Jesus's prophetic judgment was fulfilled in 70 AD, when the Roman Empire destroyed the temple and wreaked havoc on the Jewish people. Another example of foretelling in the New Testament is the prophecy of Agabus, who foretold the great famine that came upon the earth during the days of Claudius Caesar. (See Acts 11:28.)

Foretelling is a useful tool in equipping the body of Christ for significant future events. I have also seen the power of foretelling in my personal ministry. On several occasions, I have given (and received) specific words of wisdom that have affected the lives of God's people in a significant way. One day, I was prophesying over a young lady who was unemployed, and the Lord led me to tell her that He was going to turn her job situation around in the near future. I told her not to worry or fret, because God was going to open a supernatural door of employment. As the months passed, she held on to this word. All of a sudden, out of nowhere, she was offered the best job she has ever had in her career. Hallelujah!

Forth-telling

New Testament prophecy not only involves foretelling the future, but also proclaiming words of exhortation and encouragement for the present. For example, look at the apostle Peter's second epistle:

> We have also a more **sure word of prophecy**; whereunto ye do well that ye take heed, as unto a light that shineth in a dark place, until the day dawn, and the day star arise in your hearts.   (2 Peter 1:19)

In this instance, the prophetic words uttered are more of an encouragement to the church to persevere than a warning of a particular judgment or event. Peter's message was meant to edify and strengthen believers amid great testing and persecution. Prophecy is not simply the speaking of a divine message; rather the words of prophecy actually ignite our faith and stir us to action. Paul encouraged the Corinthian believers, "For we **walk by faith**, not by sight," (2 Corinthians 5:7), and again, "While we look not at the things which are seen, but at the things which are not seen: for the things which are seen are temporal; but the things which are not seen are eternal" (2 Corinthians 4:18). These prophetic reminders by the apostle Paul were meant to ignite faith in the readers and hearers and to motivate them to faith-filled action.

I want to clarify that foretelling and forth-telling is not just an Old Testament phenomenon but is also included in the job description of the New Testament prophets. We are told in 1 Corinthians 14:31, "For ye may all prophesy one by one, that all may learn, and all may be comforted." The apostle Paul uses the Greek word prophēteuō, which means "to prophesy, to be a prophet, speak forth by divine inspirations, to predict." Notice that one of the definitions here is to speak forth, or proclaim. In other words, forth-telling is the bold proclamation of divinely inspired revelation. Prophetic prayer is both the proclaiming of future events in prayer and the declaration of divine truth for the present. Either way, every believer has the grace to prophesy in some capacity.

Prophetic Prayer

Father, in the name of Jesus, I thank You for who You are and for all that You have done. I decree and declare in the name of Jesus Christ that I have the mind of Christ, according to 1 Corinthians 2:16. My mind is in perfect working order. My thoughts are the thoughts of the Holy Spirit. I take every thought captive to the obedience of Christ. My mind is renewed, according to Romans 12:2. I have a positive mental attitude. Negative thoughts cannot rule my mind. I think about the goodness, faithfulness, and provision of the Lord Jesus Christ all day long. My mind is receptive to the Word of God. I receive godly ideas that will positively impact my life and the lives of those around me. I cannot think negatively, because my mind is preoccupied with the goodness of Jesus. Lord, I thank You that my mind is consecrated to You. These things I declare in Jesus' name. Amen!

Prophetic Insights

1. What are the major differences between the prophetic nature and the prophetic office?

2. How can we access divine insight?

3. What are the two critical aspects of prophecy?

4. How would you advise someone who wanted to change his or her prayer mentality from that of a *victim* to that of a *victor*?

6

Prayer Changes Things

If two of you shall agree on earth as touching any thing that they shall ask, it shall be done for them of my Father which is in heaven.
—Matthew 18:19

If you haven't discovered it by now, let me assure you that everything in the natural realm is subject to change. This is an inescapable reality of life on the earth. And it is really great news for every believer, because it means that no difficulty, trial, or spiritual opposition is ever permanent.

The whole ethos of this book is the idea that God can change anything in our lives—He has no limitations. The Scriptures say,

> *We look not at the things which are seen, but at the things which are not seen:* **for the things which are seen are temporal;** *but the things which are not seen are eternal.* (2 Corinthians 4:18)

The word *temporal* means "for a season, enduring only for a while, temporary."

I don't know about you, but there have been seasons in my Christian walk that I thought were permanent. I once thought I would always be broke. I once thought I would always be bitter. It wasn't until I began practicing prophetic prayer that I realized just how wrong I was.

If we desire to see change and transformation in our lives, we must become people of consistent, persistent prayer. Prayer is the catalyst for change in both the spiritual and natural realm. As the older women in my church were fond of saying to me as a boy, "Prayer changes things!" In my mind, I wondered how talking to a God you couldn't see while positioned on bended knee could bring about change in your life. What I failed to understand at that time was the fact that this *invisible* God is the One who created the very *visible* universe. This is what the writer of Hebrews meant when he wrote, "*Through faith we understand that the worlds were framed by the word of God, so that things which are seen were not made of things which do appear*" (Hebrews 11:3). I like the way the *Amplified Version* expresses this verse:

> By faith we understand that the worlds [during the successive ages] were framed (fashioned, put in order, and equipped for their intended purpose) by the word of God, so that what we see was not made out of things which are visible.　　　　　(Hebrews 11:3 AMP)

If the invisible One created everything that is visible, then it makes perfect sense for us to petition Him in the invisible world for every matter pertaining to the visible world. It is a cruel irony that the visible world, with its cares and troubles, often pulls us away from the One who created it rather than pushing us closer to Him.

If you examine the Bible closely, you will see that prayer precipitated every major change throughout. For example, it was the cry of the children of Israel in their affliction that brought about their deliverance and crushed the oppressive hand of Pharaoh and his army. It was the prayer of Nehemiah that brought about revival in the city of Jerusalem after the captivity, and led to the rebuilding of the wall. It was prayer that delivered Esther and all the Jewish people from destruction during the reign of King Ahasuerus. I could offer dozens of other examples, but I think you get the idea. Prayer really does prompt change!

Why is it, then, that people don't pray the way they should? Because Satan wants the children of God to believe that their prayers are futile and fruitless. He knows that if he can get you to believe the wrong thing about prayer, that you won't pray, and ultimately you will not see the change that you desire. This is why many in the body of Christ are frustrated with God over the circumstances of their lives, never realizing that God isn't to blame.

The devil is a liar! (See John 8:44.) Give the enemy no place! (See Ephesians 4:27.) He tries to convince us that reality is limited to what we can see, touch, taste, smell, and hear. But when our minds have been changed by the Spirit of God, we know that the truest reality is not the chair we sit in or the food we eat but the God who created everything—and that's why we pray to Him instead of trusting in things or ourselves! He is the preeminent One!

PRAYER CHANGES THINGS, BEGINNING WITH YOUR MIND. A CHANGED MIND IS A CHANGED LIFE!

As believers, we should be continually conforming to the image and nature of Jesus. And we accomplish this by the renewing of our minds. A renewed mind allows us to see things differently, as well as gives us a greater consciousness of God's power. We may be born again, but unless we are constantly renewing our minds with the Word of God, studying the Word to discover who we really are, and developing our spiritual selves through prayer, the old, fleshly nature will begin to take back control!

On the other hand, when we pray and meditate on the Word of God, we are building our inner being and bringing about the change in our life that the Word has promised. This is the key to lasting change.

In our ministry, we have witnessed a total turnaround in many areas simply because we chose to pray in faith rather than complain, focus on the natural, and ignore the supernatural. Take, for example, the young man who had been addicted to nicotine for several years. He had stood in healing lines and attended a number of Christian conferences, but he always returned home in the same condition. Then he visited our church, and I prayed over him, not even knowing about the addiction he was battling. He was instantly set free from his bondage to nicotine. Over the next several days, he made numerous attempts to smoke cigarettes and found himself unable to do so. There is nothing that anyone could say to convince me that prayer is not powerful. I have seen God perform too many miracles in my life and in the lives of thousands of other people all over the world. Prayer changes things!

The Power of Agreement

One of the most powerful prayers that we can engage in is the prayer of agreement. Jesus said, *"If two of you shall agree on earth as touching any thing that they shall ask, it shall be done for them of my Father which is in heaven"* (Matthew 18:19). The Greek word for "agreement" is *symphōneō*, from which we get the English word *symphony*. To agree with someone in prayer is to come into accordance and harmony with that person regarding that which you are praying about. God is moved by agreement. Do you remember, in the book of Genesis, when the inhabitants of the earth came together to build the Tower of Babel? (See Genesis 11:4–9.) The people all spoke the same language, giving them a unity whose power was undeniable. God Himself acknowledged that whatever they sought to do would be accomplished. Ultimately, God scattered the people, and the rest is history. We can see from this biblical account that there is tremendous power in unity.

In the natural realm, synergy creates an exponential impact. The same is true in the spiritual realm. Every time we come together in faith with another person and agree to see the same outcome to our prayer, it releases supernatural synergy, which, in turn, produces exponential results. This is the reason why the enemy wants the church divided. He wants believers to be separated from one another so that we will not agree together concerning the purposes of God in the earth. He wants husbands and wives to be at odds with one another so that their prayers will be hindered. (See 1 Peter 3:7.) However, the moment we agree with others in prayer, things begin to change. If agreeing with our brothers and sisters in the body of Christ yields such powerful results, how much more powerful are the results when we come into agreement with the Word of God in prayer! Remember, the Bible says that if two people shall agree on earth concerning anything, then they will have whatever they ask for. (See Matthew 18:19.) That's wonderful! It means that once I agree with the Holy Spirit, I automatically qualify for answered prayer.

AUTHORITY IS RELEASED THROUGH PRAYER.
A PRAYERFUL PERSON IS A POWERFUL PERSON;
THE WEAKEST PERSON IS THE ONE WHO
DOESN'T PRAY.

Whatever we agree with becomes the governing force of our existence. Once we agree with God, we give His presence, power, and promises permission to dominate our lives. Too many people are not seeing change because they have refused to agree with God and His Word, instead agreeing with the lies of the enemy—lies that say positive change is not possible. Remember, our agreement determines our expectation, and our expectation determines the manifestation. Whatever we come into agreement with is what will ultimately manifest in our lives, because there is an inextricable connection between what we agree with and what changes we will see manifest. We must determine to agree only with God and endeavor to consciously identify any lies we have been believing, that we may disown them forever.

One day, I realized that I was frustrated with the direction of my life. I was tired of the lack, tired of the fear, and tired of the bondage it created. I remember saying to God, "I want change!" I wanted my life to move in a totally different direction. In my desperation, I cried out to God with what I call a "gut-level" cry.

Suddenly, I heard the Lord speak to me. He said, "I know the plans that I have toward you, My son, plans to prosper you and not to harm you!" These words, reminiscent of Jeremiah 29:11, resonated deep within my soul. I wasn't sure why, but I somehow knew that things were going to change. Prior to this encounter with God, I thought that my circumstances were the problem. But when He spoke to me, I realized that I was the problem. I needed to change. I knew that if God could change my perspective, He could change every area of my life. And that is exactly what happened. My wife and I moved from "Barely Get Along Street" to "More Than Enough Avenue."

Why did we experience such a radical shift in our circumstances? First, we simply came into agreement with the Word of God. Second, we acknowledged that God's plans were greater than the devil's plans. Finally, we made a conscious decision to walk out God's promises through prayer, faith, and obedience.

Greater than Superman

When I was a kid, one of my favorite comic-book superheroes was Superman. He could move faster than a speeding bullet. He was more powerful than a locomotive. He was able to leap over tall buildings in a single bound, see through walls, and even fly. (Ironically, the fictional superhero was inspired by the biblical figure Samson, who possessed supernatural strength from God.) Superman's alter ego was Clark Kent, a news reporter who kept a low profile and had a nondescript physical appearance. He was a sort of social archetype, representing themes like social justice and the fight against tyranny. The uniqueness of Superman was his ability to balance power with benevolence.

But even Superman is no match for the born-again, Spirit-filled believer. Jesus is greater than Superman! He said to us, *"Ye are of God, little children, and have overcome them: because **greater is he that is in you, than he that is in the world**"* (1 John 4:4). In other words, because you have Jesus living on the inside of you, you are stronger and more powerful than any comic book figure could ever be! You can leap over depression, fear, and anxiety in a single bound. You have supernatural X-ray vision to see through all the devices of the evil one. Unfortunately, most believers never tap into this supernatural dimension.

Avid fans of Superman are familiar with his "Fortress of Solitude" (also known as the "Secret Citadel"). This fortress, a secret to outsiders, was the place where Superman could retreat and be refreshed. It was also a place reminiscent of his home planet, Krypton. Like Superman, you and I must consistently retreat to our "Fortress of Solitude," the presence of God. The Bible says, *"He that dwelleth in the **secret place of the most High** shall abide under the **shadow of the Almighty**"* (Psalm 91:1). It is in the place of daily prayer and communion with God that we are energized, refreshed, and empowered to face life's challenges. As we retreat to God in prayer, we are reminded that we are not of this world but citizens of a heavenly kingdom. (See Philippians 3:20.) Hallelujah!

The Supernatural Anointing

Earlier, we said that prayer releases the supernatural. This is due to the fact that we have a supernatural anointing on the inside of us.

> But the **anointing** which ye have received of him abideth in you, and ye need not that any man teach you: but as the same **anointing** teacheth you of all things, and is truth, and is no lie, and even as it hath taught you, ye shall abide in him. (1 John 2:27)

In the Old Testament, priests were anointed with precious oil which let everyone around the priests know that these men were ordained and empowered to fulfill the priestly office. In the New Testament, the anointing manifested as the supernatural presence and power of God, equipping and empowering believers to fulfill their assignment. Unlike in the Old Testament, this anointing dwells within the believer. In other words, the anointing is the yoke-destroying, burden-removing power of God at work in and through us. The anointing inside the believer is one of the greatest gifts of the new covenant. We must learn to tap into and release this anointing on a consistent basis.

Like Superman, you and I have been endued with supernatural power. The beauty of the anointing is the fact that, unlike the temporary manifestations of the anointing on the priests and prophets of old, we carry the anointing on the inside of us twenty-four hours a day, seven days a week. We don't have to wait for a special "feeling" or an emotional experience; we can release the power of God at any time simply by praying in Jesus' name. Many times, I will walk in a room and simply say, "I release the power and presence of God in this room!" Every time I pray that way, something happens! Many believers are waiting for an encounter with God, little knowing that they are carrying that encounter on the inside. Hallelujah!

PRAYER RELEASES THE ANOINTING OF THE HOLY SPIRIT; AND WHEN THE ANOINTING IS RELEASED, MIRACLES HAPPEN!

Heavenly Downloads

As an undergraduate, I studied computer science. I was always fascinated by cutting-edge technology, so I thought it would make for a good career path. Of course, I later discovered that it was not the career path for me at all, but I did glean some very useful information along the way. While I was in school, a new technological concept called "mobile downloading" began to emerge. Now, everyone is familiar with the term "downloading"—copying data from one computer system to another, typically over the Internet. If you have a smartphone, you have probably been notified of software updates that must be *downloaded* to your mobile device via the Internet or a cellular connection. These "over-the-air" downloads allow you to receive important data on your mobile device or computer quickly and remotely.

In a similar way, the Holy Spirit wants to give us "heavenly downloads." In other words, He wants to update us with divine information, revelation, wisdom, and insight that will cause us to experience life on a higher level. Prayer is the divine connection that enables us to receive downloads from heaven into our spiritual being. As with all technological devices, updating the software creates a totally different user experience. It enables the device to do things it could not do before. In the same way, prayer empowers us to do things we couldn't do before, and to experience changes in areas we never dreamed could be altered.

The apostle Paul knew all about receiving downloads from God, especially in his most difficult times. In one instance, God warned Paul, via a download from the Holy Spirit, of the peril that he would face on his journey via a download from the Holy Spirit. *"Now when much time was spent, and when sailing was now dangerous, because the fast was now already past, Paul admonished them, and said unto them, Sirs, I perceive that this voyage will be with hurt and much damage, not only of the lading and ship, but also of our lives"* (Acts 27:9–10). How many areas of our lives could use a download of heavenly data via prayer!

Spiritual Encoding and Decoding

For many people, the real issue when it comes to hearing God's voice is determining which voice is actually the voice of God. How do we know when we are hearing from God? In all communication, there is something called encoding and decoding. What do we mean by the terms encoding and decoding? Simply put, encoding is the process of converting information into coded form, and decoding is the process of converting an encoded message into intelligible language. Imagine talking on a cell phone: every time you speak into the cell phone microphone, your voice is encoded into data, which is then transmitted over a cellular signal. Once that data reaches the person on the other end of the phone, it is then decoded from digital signals into intelligible language. Every time we hear something, there must be a conversion of that sound or information into a form that we can process and understand.

The same is true in the spiritual realm! We must learn to decipher what God is saying. Many times the Holy Spirit will speak to us in the form of a thought or an impression. Other times, the Spirit may speak us through a Scripture or even through an audible voice. God may not speak to us the same way every time, but we must learn how to decode His voice. The key to decoding the voice of God is the Word of God, because God will never say anything that contradicts His Word. The more we meditate in the Word of God, the more we will be able to decipher what the Holy Spirit is speaking to us.

GOD SPEAKS TO THE BELIEVER IN MANY DIFFERENT WAYS, BUT IT WILL ALWAYS ALIGN WITH THE WORD OF GOD.

One day, while in college, I was sitting in the cafeteria with a friend of mine when a young lady came up and sat down next to us at the table. As my friend began to speak to her about the Lord, I kept getting this impression about the number six. Every time I looked at this young lady, I would "hear" the word *six* inside my head. Finally, I mustered the courage to ask her, "Did something happen when you were six?" She looked startled, and then responded, "Yes!" I gently asked, "What happened when you were six?" She proceeded to share a very traumatic experience with us. We prayed for her and told her about the love of Christ. She was dumbfounded that I knew about such an intimate detail of her life. I only knew, however, because I followed the still, small voice within. The number six was like a code that I had to decipher in order to hear what God was speaking concerning the young lady to whom we ministered. I have since learned that God doesn't always want us to repeat out loud something that He reveals to our hearts, but He did teach me in that moment at the cafeteria this valuable lesson: I must develop a sensitivity to the voice of God. The more we as believers learn to be sensitive, the more we will be able to recognize His voice when He speaks. I want to share the following prayer with you because I believe it will help you to become more sensitive to the Holy Spirit.

Prophetic Prayer

Father, I thank You that Your Word is the final authority in my life. I acknowledge the fact that You are alive within me. I thank You that my righteousness is not based on religious works but on Your power and grace. I confess that Jesus Christ is the Lord of my life. All my validation, worth, and acceptance come from You, Lord Jesus. From this day forward, I walk in the power of the Holy Spirit. I am not controlled by religion, but I am free to serve You in truth. You speak to me, Lord, in a still, small voice, and I hear it and decode it according to Your Word. You spread mercy and love through Your words to my heart. May I never reject Your Spirit! In Jesus' name, amen!

Prophetic Insights

1. What are some examples from the Bible and/or from your own life when prayer changed things?

2. What does God's anointing look like today?

3. Have you ever received a "heavenly download"?

PROPHETIC PRACTICUM

1. Remember that every time you meditate on the Word of God, you are looking into God's heart. Ask God to allow His emotions to be your emotions, so you might feel what He feels and then share that with others.

2. Have you ever prayed for longer than five or ten minutes? If not, consider setting aside an hour to come before Jesus—no distractions; nobody else but you and God. Instead of filling the time by making requests, ask God to download divine "data" into your spiritual self. Pray specifically for the people and situations He reveals to you.

3. You don't have to wait for a feeling or an emotion to confirm God's presence, because you carry the anointing inside of you twenty-four hours a day, seven days a week. This week, walk into a room and simply say, "I release the power and presence of God in this room!"

7

Prophetic Decrees

*Thou shalt also **decree a thing**, and it shall be established unto thee:*
and the light shall shine upon thy ways.
—Job 22:28

O ne of the most important steps in prophetic prayer is making prophetic decrees. What is a prophetic decree? The Bible tells us in Job
22:28, *"Thou shalt decree a thing, and it shall be established."* The word *"decree"*
here comes from the Hebrew word *gazar*, which means "to divide, cut down,
or snatch." Like a lumberjack cutting through a forest with an ax to make a
path, prophetic decrees have the power to cut down the things that don't belong in our lives, creating a pathway of miracles in their place. This is a divine
principle that the Lord began to reveal to me many years ago. Before this
time, I would simply pray passively, then sit around and wait for something
to happen. If nothing seemed to be happening in the natural, I automatically
assumed that God hadn't heard my prayer or had decided not to answer it.

You can probably imagine the frustration I experienced in this cycle of
seemingly ineffective prayers. That is, until the Lord showed me that I had

a part to play in the outcome of my prayers. I didn't have to just sit back and "let life happen." Rather, I could assume an active role and use my prayers to affect the outcomes of situations and circumstances.

Too many believers are ignorant of the profound power of the Word of God. When the Bible talks about making decrees, it is not making an idle statement. Prophetic decrees are faith-filled words based on the revealed Word of God, and released from the mouths of born-again believers. I am reminded of the story of Abraham and his son Isaac. God instructed Abraham to take his son on a journey in preparation for sacrificing him on an altar. (See Genesis 22:2.) Instead of protesting, Abraham responded in faith, not knowing what God was up to. The Bible records what happened next:

> *And Isaac spake unto Abraham his father, and said, My father: and he said, Here am I, my son. And he said, Behold the fire and the wood: but where is the lamb for a burnt offering? And Abraham said, My son, God will provide himself a lamb for a burnt offering: so they went both of them together.* (Genesis 22:7–8)

Notice that Abraham spoke in faith concerning the outcome of this situation. He told his son that God would provide a lamb. He never said, "I am about to kill you, son!" Even though God told him to sacrifice Isaac, and even though he didn't see a physical lamb, Abraham knew the nature of God, and therefore, he was able to make a prophetic decree about God's supernatural provision. God provided a lamb according to the word of Abraham. That is the power of prophetic decrees!

EVERY TIME WE SPEAK GOD'S WORD,
WE ARE AGREEING WITH GOD AND
RELEASING HIS POWER!

One day, I was talking to a friend of mine who also happens to be a fellow minister. We prayed together about some issues that my family and I were facing in ministry. After we were finished praying, my friend suddenly said, "The Lord is going to give you twenty thousand dollars!" He then laughed and exclaimed that he didn't know where that statement had come from! I said "Amen," and thanked him for sharing those words with me. Several days later, I began to declare that God was going to bless me with at least $20,000 that same month. (You must learn to agree with prophecy if you want to see a prophetic statement manifest in your life.) Several weeks later, someone wrote my wife and me a check for over $20,000. Praise God! My friend's statement hadn't sounded like a formal prophetic word when he'd spoken it, but it turned out to be a prophetic decree that God was about to turn things around in our favor.

When we understand the power of prophetic decrees, we cease to engage in what I call "reactive prayer"—praying reactionary prayers in response to the circumstances of our lives. We tend to react when we see ourselves as victims rather than victors. We must refuse to be reactive, and be proactive, in Jesus' name! We should determine the outcome of every circumstance well before it materializes.

Speaking Spirits

Whether you know it or not, we are speaking, spiritual beings with the capacity to either create or destroy with our words. This is not a New Age concept; it is a biblical truth about which most Christians are ignorant. Again, the Bible says, "**God is a Spirit**: *and they that worship him must worship him in* **spirit** *and in truth*" (John 4:24). When God created man, He created him in His image and after His likeness. (See Genesis 1:26.) God is a speaking Spirit; therefore, mankind has inherited a speaking spirit. What does that mean, exactly? The Bible says in Genesis 1,

> *In the beginning God created the heaven and the earth. And the earth was without form, and void; and darkness was upon the face of the deep. And the Spirit of God moved upon the face of the waters.* ***And God said, Let there be light: and there was light.*** (Genesis 1:1–3)

We can understand from this passage that God created the physical world through His spoken Word. In a similar fashion, we create our "world" through the words that we speak. Have you ever taken inventory of the words that you speak every day? You would probably be amazed by the correlation between the words you speak and the condition of your life.

By speaking the natural world into existence, God was setting a prophetic precedent for every born-again believer. It seems as though the New Age community has hijacked this very powerful principle from the church. Contrary to New Age philosophy, the idea of speaking things into existence was never meant to work outside the context of Christianity.

One of the first assignments that God gave to Adam, the first man on the earth, was to name the animals. Genesis 2:19 says,

> And out of the ground the LORD God formed every beast of the field, and every fowl of the air; and brought them unto Adam to see what he would call them: and whatsoever Adam called every living creature, that was the name thereof.

The word for *"called"* in this verse is the Hebrew word *qara'*, which means "to utter a loud sound, to proclaim." In other words, whatever Adam proclaimed in the earth was established in the earth. He was, in essence, making prophetic proclamations over the animal kingdom. Whatever he called the animals, that was their name! This is an idiomatic expression (from the Hebrew word *shem*) that suggests Adam was establishing the nature, character, and function of every creature in the earth. What an amazing process! Through the spoken word, Adam framed the garden environment.

The Power of Proclamation

What if it were possible for you and me to do the same thing that Adam did?

Guess what? It *is* possible! We don't need to name the animals, as Adam did, but we can "name" the situations and circumstances in our lives. We can make prophetic proclamations, like Adam did in the garden of Eden, and watch the power of God transform our world accordingly. We can't live a life of power and victory in silence, for a life of power and victory demands words. We must speak! We must open our mouths and proclaim the Word of God over our children, our finances, our health, our ministries, our communities, and every other area of our lives. In essence, we have to dictate our circumstances instead of allowing our circumstances to dictate the nature of our lives.

After one church service, a mother and her daughter came to me, both with tears in their eyes. As they explained, the daughter was facing a serious prison sentence. She was absolutely devastated. The news was particularly upsetting to me when I learned that this young lady had a daughter of her own, who, if the young woman were to be convicted and sentenced, would become a ward of the state. I knew that this was not the will of God, so I began to pray for this young woman. I made a prophetic proclamation that the judge would grant her unusual favor. I proclaimed that he would look at her through different eyes. I declared that the court case would be thrown out, in Jesus' name! Several months later, we discovered that the woman had not been sentenced to time in prison. She was exonerated! Hallelujah! There is power in proclamation.

There are times when we should ask God to show us His will concerning specific situations, but there are also times when we don't need to ask God what His will is; we simply need to proclaim His Word in faith and with boldness. When we talk about making prophetic decrees or proclamations, we are referring to faith-filled words that we speak out from our spirit (or inner being). The Bible tells us, *"Of the abundance of the heart* [inner being] *his* [a person's] *mouth speaketh"* (Luke 6:45). When our faith connects with the words spoken from our heart, it becomes a formula for manifestation.

BE CAREFUL WHAT YOU SAY!
WHATEVER WE SPEAK FROM THE HEART IN FAITH
WILL MANIFEST IN OUR LIVES!

The Bible tells us very clearly that we will have what we say! If we don't want it, we shouldn't say it. This is oftentimes easier said than done, because we live in a society that is pervaded by negativity. Everywhere we turn, there seems to be a flood of fear, doubt, unbelief, and despair. This is why we must make a conscious decision to meditate on the Word of God and to pray in order to transcend the negative atmosphere. We don't have to adopt the attitude of the rest of the world. Every morning when we get up, we must declare: "Today is a day of miracles! Everything will work in my favor, in Jesus' name!" Don't subject yourself to the atmosphere around you; instead, change the atmosphere through the Word of God.

Speak to the Mountain

There is no greater example of the power of prophetic decrees than the example that was set by our Lord Himself. Jesus lived in a state of constant communion and fellowship with the Father. In fact, prayer was His top priority. In a sense, Jesus lived in His own world—a world in which God's Word had the final authority. We know that Jesus was fully God, but He was also fully man, which means that you and I, as human beings created in His image, can live in that same world.

Mark's gospel includes the following example—an unusual encounter between Jesus and a fig tree:

And on the morrow, when [Jesus and His disciples] *were come from Bethany,* [Jesus] *was hungry: and seeing a fig tree afar off having leaves, he came, if haply he might find any thing thereon: and when he came to it, he found nothing but leaves; for the time of figs was not yet. And Jesus answered and said unto it, No man eat fruit of thee hereafter forever. And his disciples heard it.* (Mark 11:12–14)

The next morning, Peter saw that the roots of the fig tree had dried up, and he brought it to Jesus' attention. To this, Jesus responded,

Have faith in God. For verily I say unto you, That whosoever shall say unto this mountain, Be thou removed, and be thou cast into the sea; and shall not doubt in his heart, but shall believe that those things which he saith shall come to pass; he shall have whatsoever he saith. (Mark 11:22–23)

The word for *"saith"* here is the Greek word *eipon*, which means "to make known one's thoughts, to declare." Jesus was telling the disciples, in other words, "Whenever you make a faith-filled declaration with your mouth, mountains *must* move."

What are some of the "mountains" in your life that need to move today? Do you believe that the Word of God is more powerful than the situation you are facing? Notice that Jesus stressed the importance of believing that what we say *"shall come to pass."* This is critical when it comes to prophetic prayer. We must have conviction, based on God's Word, that what we declare will surely manifest. The enemy wants us to doubt that what we say will happen. This is why many people pray—and then worry! They don't really believe that things are going to work out in their favor. But God wants us to know, beyond the shadow of a doubt, that He has heard our prayer—be it one of supplication or of declaration—and that it is just a matter of time before we will see the full manifestation of that prayer.

Further Lessons from the Fig Tree

In the account I just shared from the gospel of Mark, did you notice that Jesus walked away after cursing the fig tree? He didn't wait around to see if anything would happen. He didn't stress or toil over the tree. Why? Because He knew that the moment He spoke, it was already done. As far as heaven was concerned, that fig tree was dead the moment Jesus cursed it!

How different would our lives look if we believed with all our heart that the moment we spoke something, it was already done? There is a powerful lesson to be learned from the account of Jesus and the fig tree. It may be a challenge to wrap our minds around this concept, because many religious leaders teach us, in effect, that our words ultimately have no meaning. This is simply not true! Jesus said, *"The words that I speak unto you, they are spirit, and they are life"* (John 6:63). The Greek term for *"life"* in this verse is *zōē*, "life real and genuine, a life active and vigorous." Our words, like Jesus' words, contain creative power. The fig tree represented something that should have been fruitful but instead was barren. Perhaps there are areas in your life that are barren, just like that fig tree. Your response should be the same as Jesus': speak to them!

During an evening healing meeting, the Holy Spirit gave me a word of knowledge about physical abuse. I proclaimed it, and, after much hesitation, a young lady came down to the front and confessed that she was in an abusive relationship. In addition to suffering physical and emotional abuse, she had discovered several lumps on her breast and underarm. Typically, I would have laid hands on the woman's shoulders or asked another female to help me to pray for the woman, commanding that she be healed. But this time, the Holy Spirit told me not to lay hands on this woman. Instead, the Lord said, "Just speak to her! Tell her that she shall not die but live." And that is exactly what I did! I told the young woman that she would not die but live, and I cursed the cancerous growths on her body. Within minutes, the woman came back to me with tears in her eyes and exclaimed, "I can't believe it—the tumors are gone!" Glory to God! The spoken Word of God is pregnant with God's miraculous power!

EVERY AREA OF DEPRIVATION WILL BE FILLED WHEN WE SPEAK THE LIVING WORD OF GOD!

Blessings and Curses

Throughout the Bible, we see a very powerful principle at work: the principle of blessings and curses. In Deuteronomy 28, God established the blessings and curses that would come upon Israel according to their response to His divine laws. If they kept God's covenant, they were blessed; if they rejected God's covenant, they were cursed.

The word for *"blessing"* (or "blessed") in Deuteronomy 29 is the Hebrew word *bĕrakah*, which means "prosperity or peace." The root of this word, *barak*, means "to cause to kneel." This blessing was an oral pronunciation over Israel that produced favor, prosperity, peace, and protection.

Deuteronomy 28:8 reads, "*The* LORD *shall command the blessing upon thee in thy storehouses, and in all that thou settest thine hand unto; and he shall bless thee in the land which the* LORD *thy God giveth thee.*" The word "*command*" means to "lay charge, give orders, or to commission." In other words, God spoke, or declared, a blessing over the Israelites—a blessing that commissioned prosperity to flow into the lives of the people of Israel. A curse is the antithesis of a blessing; to curse something means to speak or charge evil on someone or something.

Under the new covenant, believers have the ability to release either blessings or curses out of their mouths. Jesus says to us, "*Love your enemies, bless them that curse you, do good to them that hate you, and pray for them which despitefully use you, and persecute you*" (Matthew 5:44). The Greek word for "*bless*" in this verse, *eulogeō*, is a transliteration of the Hebrew word *barak*. Every time we speak favorably toward someone, we are blessing that person; and every time we speak evil of someone, we are cursing that person. There is a direct correlation between what we speak out of our mouths and whether we are walking in the blessings of God. Jesus died on the cross to abolish the curse that hovered over us (see Galatians 3:13–14); therefore, we ought to speak only blessings over others and ourselves.

What You Say Is What You Get!

Few people recognize the magnitude of the power of the words they speak on a consistent basis. Many years ago, the Lord began to give me a revelation about the profound effect of our words on our destiny. One day, while watching a popular Christian television program, I said to myself, *I am going to be on that show!* Several months later, a representative from that show called me and asked if I would be willing to fly to their studio location and film an interview. Wow! How did that happen? Simply put, I spoke it! And that wasn't the only time I had such an experience.

Jesus said, "*The words that I speak unto you, they are **spirit**, and they are **life**"* (John 6:63). The words we speak are literally alive. All born-again believers have the divine capacity to speak life or death, blessing or cursing, because they carry the "*zōē*" of God on the inside. I want to submit to you that what you say is exactly what you get! If you want to examine where your life is headed, you only need to take inventory of the words you are speaking on a regular basis.

Unfortunately, many Christians believe that the idea of receiving that which one speaks is a New Age practice. They don't recognize that the New Age worldview is a perversion and a distortion of biblical principles. Remember, when Jesus cursed the fig tree, it died. Why? Because the Word of God is living and active, and pregnant with the power of God.

I once discovered a growth on my leg. At first, I thought it was a scab from a previous wound, but after it refused to go away, I became concerned. I showed it to my wife, and her answer surprised me: "Just curse it!" I don't know why I hadn't thought of that before, but I began to do exactly as she'd suggested. I began to command the growth to wither and die, like the fig tree in the eleventh chapter of Mark. After some time, I noticed that the growth had withered away. Praise God!

Whatever we speak in faith is what we are going to receive. This means that we need to very careful about the things we say. Remember, we are prophetic in nature; therefore, we have to make sure that the things we declare with our mouths are in accordance with the Word of God. If we don't want to be sick, we should stop saying, "I'm sick"! If we don't want to be broke, we must stop claiming our lack and poverty.

We prayed for a young lady at our church and declared that God would use her to heal the sick. At the same time, we also prayed for a man who had terminal cancer. His doctor had given him three months to live. Shortly after we prayed for this man, the young lady for whom we had prayed went to visit him in the hospital and prayed over him, declaring that he would receive a miracle *now*! The following week, the doctor reported that the man's cancer was in remission. Glory to God! Christ is still the Healer!

Prophetic Prayer

Father, in the name of Jesus, I thank You for who You are and for all You have done. Right now, in the name of Jesus, I decree and declare that I have great *faith*. In accordance with Mark 11:22–23, I have the faith of God, and every mountain in my life and in the lives of those around me must obey my voice. I open my mouth right now and I say that doubt and unbelief must depart from me. I am a believer in the Word of God. Every Word in the Bible is the truth, and I believe it. The Word of God is the final authority in my life. I am not moved by what I see, but I am moved by the Word of God alone. I walk by faith in the Word of God and not by sight. I am not controlled by my emotions, the emotions of others, or my environment, but I am completely dominated by God's Word. Romans 10:17 declares that faith comes by hearing, and hearing by the Word of God. I am a hearer of Your Word, oh Lord; and as a result, I have faith. Faith is the revelation of God's Word in action; therefore, I am a doer of Your Word. Nothing is impossible to me, because I am a believer in Your Word. I declare that I have a positive outlook on life, today and every day. I see the best in myself and in those around me. I have an optimistic attitude because the Word of God declares in Philippians 4:13 that I can do all things through Christ who strengthens me. I declare that I am strong. I am successful. I am filled with the fullness of God. Today is a day in which I will demonstrate the goodness of God through my positive mental attitude. In Jesus' name, amen!

Prophetic Insights

1. Where is your life headed, according to the words you speak on a regular basis?

2. What does the account of Jesus and the fig tree in Mark 11 teach us about the power of our words?

3. What promises from the Bible can you declare over your life today?

8

Binding and Loosing

And I will give unto thee the keys of the kingdom of heaven: and whatsoever thou shalt bind on earth shall be bound in heaven: and whatsoever thou shalt loose on earth shall be loosed in heaven.
—Matthew 16:19

You may have heard someone say, "Devil, I bind you, in Jesus' name!" Years ago, I heard a story about a preacher who tried to cast a demon out of a man in his church. He told the man, "Satan, I bind you, in Jesus' name!" After he did this, the man spoke some offensive words to the pastor, and the pastor responded with physical force. He actually began beating the man. So much for binding the devil!

This story may sound funny, but it is an accurate depiction of the uninformed way many believers approach the devil and spiritual warfare. Many people in the body of Christ are unaware of the power and authority they possess in both the spiritual and earthly realms. The Bible says that we have received the keys to the kingdom of heaven. (See Matthew 16:19.) What are the keys to the kingdom of heaven? First, consider the nature of a key—something that grants its holder access to a specific place. Keys always correspond to the grounds where they belong. In this case, the keys we have received as new covenant believers correspond to the kingdom of heaven. This is why Jesus said, *"Whatever you bind on earth will be bound in heaven, and whatever you loose on earth will be loosed in heaven"* (Matthew 16:19 NKJV).

Everything we do in the earthly realm causes a corresponding response in the heavenly realm, and vice versa. The word *"bind"* in Matthew 16:19, *deō*, means "to put under obligation of law, to forbid, prohibit, or declare to be illicit." In other words, we have been given the legal authority to bind things, situations, and demonic forces to the law of heaven, which is the Word of God. The reason we can bind the enemy is because he comes under the jurisdiction of the kingdom of heaven. Through Christ, we are the legal representatives, or ambassadors, of the kingdom of God on earth.

WHATEVER WE PERMIT IN THE EARTH WILL BE PERMITTED IN HEAVEN. WHEN WE DECIDE WHAT WE CANNOT TOLERATE, HEAVEN WILL COME INTO AGREEMENT.

I once worked as an insurance agent. Having been trained in agency law, I was very familiar with the term "fiduciary duty"; it means that the agent is bound by law to act on behalf of the agency he or she represents. Because of fiduciary duty, the agency can assume that all actions of the agent are in the best interests of the agency. In the same way, any spiritual forces will assume that when we say something in Jesus' name, we are acting on behalf of the kingdom of heaven. Therefore, when we speak, heaven responds! This is what it means to bind the enemy. We are telling the kingdom of darkness that it is violating its legal jurisdiction. This is not just some empty jargon that we use in church. Once we grab hold of the revelation of our authority in Christ, we can cause demons to flee just by speaking a few words!

The process of loosing demonic forces follows the same logic. The word *"loose"* in Matthew 16:19 comes from the Greek word *lyō*, which means "to unbind,…dismiss,…dissolve,…annul,…declare unlawful." The word picture is that of a police officer dismantling an unlawful assembly. Whenever an angry mob is gathered, the police have the authority and responsibility to break up that mob just by saying, "Disperse, now!" In the same way, we have the authority in Christ to release demons from their assignment, which is to scatter ungodly activity in our lives. The word *"loose"* has another meaning—to release. This means that we can release things (including healing, blessings, and prosperity) into our lives and the lives of others just by the words we speak.

Binding Demonic Activity

I was once traveling by plane from Tampa to the United Kingdom, with a scheduled layover in Atlanta. We were about to land in Atlanta when the pilot came over the intercom and said that he needed to wait until a wind shear over the landing strip had cleared. We circled in the air for thirty minutes, and I knew that if this went on for much longer, I would likely miss my connector flight to Manchester. So, I decided to ask God what was going on. The Lord spoke to me and said, "Kynan, you know you can speak to this situation, right?" Then He said, "Speak to the principality that's preventing you from landing." After this, I closed my eyes and saw a large tarantula—it was the size of the entire airport!—hovering over the landing strip. I began to take authority over this demonic spirit, commanding the power of the principality to be broken. Once I did, I saw in the spiritual realm a huge ax chop the tarantula into pieces. Hallelujah! The Lord then said to me, "Now, land the plane!" So, I prayed a simple prayer: "Plane, land, in Jesus' name!" Before I could even say "Amen," the pilot announced over the intercom, "We are about to land right now!" Glory to God! You and I have been given authority over the principalities and powers that operate in the atmospheric region.

JUST AS A KEY UNLOCKS A PHYSICAL DOOR, OUR WORDS UNLOCK DOORS TO DIVINE ACTIVITY IN OUR LIVES.

The Bible records a very profound testimony of a woman who was bound by a demonic spirit of infirmity:

And, behold, there was a woman which had a spirit of infirmity eigh-teen years, and was bowed together, and could in no wise lift up her-self. And when Jesus saw her, he called her to him, and said unto her, Woman, thou art loosed from thine infirmity.   (Luke 13:11–12)

Jesus recognized by the Holy Spirit that this woman's condition was attributable to demonic activity. The term "spirit of infirmity" refers to any spirit or condition that cannot be medically explained. Jesus proclaimed, *"Woman, thou art loosed"* and laid His hands on her, thereby setting her free—instantly and completely.

On a mission trip to Liberia, I encountered a young lady bound by a spirit of infirmity. She was full of despair and hopelessness. As I minis-tered at one of the evening meetings, the Lord drew my attention to this young woman. I told the ushers to call her forward so that I could pray with her. I commanded the spirit of infirmity and death to be broken off her, and then I laid my hands upon her head. She began to scream and cry. She fell to the ground, writhing in agony, and suddenly she was set free by the power of God. Two days later, she came to meet with me and the host pastor. She told us how the Spirit of God had set her free from depression and despair, and that she felt for the first time in her life that she had a purpose. Hallelujah! Look at what God can do!

The Power of Divine Alignment

Earlier, we discovered that God has given us, His church, the keys to the kingdom of heaven. It is important to note that the Bible says *"keys"* (plural) rather than *"key"* (singular). The reason it uses the plural form is because different keys are required to unlock different doors. There are doors of healing, doors of favor, doors of blessing, and doors of break-through that we need to unlock in order to fully enjoy the benefits of the new covenant. And all these keys function according to the principle of alignment. In other words, the particular pattern of the key is meant to align with the pattern inside the lock. When the right key meets the right lock, there is a release, and the door is opened.

In the same way, you and I, as believers, need to align our thoughts, words, and actions with heaven if we want to unlock the door to the supernatural in our lives. We do this by coming into agreement with the Word of God. The Bible says,

> *That if thou shalt confess with thy mouth the Lord Jesus, and shalt believe in thine heart that God hath raised him from the dead, thou shalt be saved. For with the heart man believeth unto righteousness; and with the mouth confession is made unto salvation.*   (Romans 10:9–10)

When the heart and the mouth align, something supernatural happens. Many people say things they don't really believe. For example, they may say they're healed, but they still believe they're sick. They may say they are prosperous, but, deep inside, they still believe they are broke. Beloved, what we say and what we believe must become one if we want to experience real breakthrough. Therefore, when we pray, we must come into alignment with God's written Word. The Word of God says we are blessed, so we ought to declare that we are blessed, no matter what our bank statements may say. By confessing the Word of God and believing its truth with all our heart, we align the key in the lock and position ourselves for breakthrough and total turnaround. What we believe is what we will speak, and what we speak is what we will ultimately act upon!

Unlocking the Heavens

The Bible tells us in the book of Malachi,

> *Bring ye all the tithes into the storehouse, that there may be meat in mine house, and prove me now herewith, saith the LORD of hosts, if I will not open you the **windows of heaven**, and pour you out a blessing, that there shall not be room enough to receive it.*   (Malachi 3:10)

What does it mean to "open the windows of heaven"? In the Hebrew, the word for *"windows"* here can mean "lattice"—a type of ornamental window that in ancient times was found only in the residences of royalty and other wealthy individuals. How fitting that God, the King of the universe, would have lattice windows! But the windows mentioned in this verse open from heaven, representing God's unlimited provision, blessings, and favor. In other words, the verse is telling us that God will open up His expansive reservoir and pour out a blessing in such a way that there will not be enough room for us to contain it! Hallelujah!

Notice that this blessing corresponds with the actions of people on the earth. As long as the Israelites were faithful in giving tithes and offerings, God unlocked the heavens and poured out His supernatural blessing upon them. I don't know about you, but that sounds good to me! And the best part? The same can be true of you and me today! When we align ourselves with God's Word, heaven responds, and there is a release of supernatural breakthrough. In the Scriptures, God says, *"If my people, which are called by my name, shall humble themselves, and pray, and seek my face, and turn from their wicked ways; then will I **hear from heaven**, and will forgive their sin, and will heal their land"* (2 Chronicles 7:14).

Our prayers have the power to move heaven, and our faith and obedience release the blessing of God in our lives. Just like a key unlocks a door, our prayers, faith, and obedience unlock the heavens. Beloved, it is possible to live under an open heaven all the days of our lives.

WHEN WE COME INTO ALIGNMENT WITH HEAVEN, AND RECOGNIZE THAT GOD'S WILL FOR US IS GOOD, WE WILL BEGIN TO WALK IN THE ACCELERATED MANIFESTATION OF GOD'S PROMISES TO US.

Again, the Bible tells us in Luke 10:19 that we have received authority from the Lord Jesus Himself. What does this imply? As I mentioned before, in insurance law, the agent carries the same authority as the one he or she represents. In other words, when we pray, we are operating in the same authority as Jesus Himself. This is what it really means to pray in Jesus' name. We possess the ability to open the heavens through prayer!

> Now then we are **ambassadors** for Christ, as though God did beseech you by us: we pray you in Christ's stead, be ye reconciled to God.
>
> (2 Corinthians 5:20)

All spiritual authority comes from the revelation of Jesus Christ (that is, the Word of God). The more revelation we have, the more authority we will wield. Can you imagine praying the same way Jesus prayed? Can you imagine getting the same results to your prayers as Jesus did? It may seem too good to be true, but this is exactly what is available to us, as new covenant believers in Jesus. Most Christians don't recognize the spiritual authority they have; therefore, they don't pray with boldness or confidence.

We must never pray with the mentality that we are victims of our circumstances. This type of mentality is rooted in powerlessness and fear, and it will ultimately undermine the effectiveness of our prayer life. Prophetic prayer is all about the authority of the believer and the power of God's Word. When we pray, we must release our faith in the power of God, and be confident that God has heard us.

What would you think if you were pulled over by a police officer, and he said to you, "Please don't be offended, but may I please see your driver's license? I am so sorry to bother you today; however, I think you might have committed a traffic violation"? You would probably be very disturbed—and maybe you wouldn't even trust him! Why? Because you expect every officer of the law to be confident of his or her authority. In the same way, you and I, as "spiritual officers" in the earth, should be confident of the authority that we possess in Christ. We should rest assured that when we command Satan to go, he has to leave. Nothing will change in our lives until we have learned to pray with this kind of authority.

Breaking the Spirit of Prevention

Several years ago, I traveled with a team to Haiti on a mission trip to preach the gospel and feed hundreds of children. Once we landed in

Port-au-Prince, we traveled by jeep toward a city called Port-de-Paix, high in the mountains. The trip was very difficult, with the already rough roads made more hazardous by the devastating earthquake of 2010. On our way up the mountain, one of our jeeps broke down. This posed a serious problem because there was not a single mechanic within a sixty-mile radius.

The only thing that we could do was pray, and I am very glad we did. As I have said before, prayer is God's means of bringing supernatural solutions to our problems. When we began to pray, the Lord said to me, "Worship!" Obediently, I began to sing songs to the Lord. Several of the other missionaries joined in; and before we knew it, the jeep came to life again.

How is it that worship "fixed" a mechanical problem in a motor vehicle? The truth is that it wasn't just a mechanical problem; it was a spiritual problem. The enemy was trying to hinder us from reaching our destination because he understood the potential impact of our assignment. He knew that many people would be saved, healed, and delivered through our work in Haiti.

The jeep's failure was due to what we would call a "hindering spirit" or a "spirit of prevention," or any spirit that attempts to keep believers from moving forward in the purpose and plan of God for their lives. This type of spirit tries to attack our health, our finances, our ministries, and so forth, with the goal of bringing fear, discouragement, and frustration.

The apostle Paul acknowledged this very spirit in his epistle to the Thessalonian church when he wrote, "*Wherefore we would have come unto you, even I Paul, once and again; but Satan hindered us*" (1 Thessalonians 2:18). The word "*hindered*" comes from the Greek word *egkoptō*, which means "to impede one's course by cutting off his way." Paul intended to come to the Thessalonians, but he was blocked by a spiritual force.

Have you ever had the sense that something (other than yourself) was holding up your rightful blessings? This may very well have been an instance of a spirit of prevention at work! Now, it is important to note that Satan has no *real* power to stop anything that God has ordained for your life; however, he nonetheless seeks to distract you from God's purposes by throwing roadblocks and diversions in your path. Once you recognize that a spirit of prevention is at work, you can take authority over that spirit, in Jesus' name.

The key to breaking free from a spirit of prevention is to pray without ceasing and to stand in faith on the Word of God.

You Are Not a Victim

I want you to imagine that you have access to any information that you desire, at any time. What would you do? Now, imagine that you have access to *supernatural* power twenty-four hours a day. What would you accomplish?

Well, I want you to absorb the truth that you *do* have access to supernatural power and supernatural information—and that access is called *prayer*! When you truly receive the revelation of prophetic prayer and embrace it with all your heart, you will never be a victim again. A praying person can never be a victim. The more we pray, the more we will walk in victory. When we are people of prayer, life doesn't "happen to us" or catch us by surprise, because we are always in the know. We are always ten steps ahead of the devil.

Let me share with you another powerful story. While in prayer, a prominent pastor in Africa was told by the Holy Spirit that armed robbers were coming for him and his family. After he heard this warning, he began to pray in the Holy Spirit. He bound up the spirit of murder and violence. Then he went to his family and staff and told them that armed robbers were going to attempt to rob him, but not to worry, because "I have dealt with them in prayer!" Several hours later, he received word that a group of armed men had been killed in a car accident. They had died around the same time he'd been praying in his house. I have learned that it is not wise to mess with a praying person! I am not suggesting that we pray for people to die in car accidents, but I am saying that prayer is more powerful than you can ever imagine.

I have had my share of phenomenal encounters. Once, a woman came all the way from Mississippi to our healing school in Tampa. She was desperate to be healed. We led the entire school in a prayer of release from anger and bitterness. This woman was instantly healed of fibromyalgia and chronic migraine headaches. Praise the name of Jehovah, for He is truly our Healer!

In our church, we pray a special prayer of healing and deliverance over any person who is ill, hospitalized, has received a negative diagnosis, or is experiencing lying symptoms in his or her body. We declare that this person is healed, set free, delivered, and restored by the stripes of Jesus, according to 1 Peter 2:24. We curse cancer, diabetes, stroke, end-stage renal disease, heart disease, heart attack, Crohn's disease, lupus, MS, HIV/AIDS, lung disease, and any other illness, affliction, or oppression (physical, spiritual, emotional, or otherwise) in the name of Jesus, and command the power, peace, and restoration of God to manifest immediately. We release the healing power of Jesus now. Let me encourage you: pray in Jesus' name with all those you love!

PRAYER HAS THE POWER TO ALTER THE FABRIC OF REALITY.

Prophetic Prayer

Father, in the name of Jesus, I declare that every hindering spirit that would produce lack, stagnation, drought, barrenness, and prevention is broken. I declare that the anointing of Jesus Christ destroys every yoke of bondage and removes every burden in my life right now! All locusts, cankerworms, and devouring spirits are cast out, rebuked, bound, and forbidden, in Jesus' name, according to Matthew 16:19. Whatever we bind on earth is bound in heaven, and whatever we loose on earth is loosed in heaven. In the name of Jesus, I loose the peace, provision, promotion, prosperity, and power of God in every area of my life. I embrace and step into the anointing for acceleration, increase, and manifestation, from this day forward. In Jesus' name, amen!

Prophetic Insights

1. What are the keys to the kingdom of heaven, and how can we use them?

2. Where does your spiritual authority come from?

3. Have you ever seen the spirit of hindrance at work in your life?

PROPHETIC PRACTICUM

1. The Word of God has a lot to say about the specific areas of our lives, including marriage and families (see, for example, Psalm 127:3–5; Matthew 19:14; Ephesians 5), health (see, for example, Psalm 41; 3 John 1:2), ministries (see, for example, Matthew 28:18–20; Acts 9:31), and community (see, for example, Romans 13:1–7; 1 Peter 2:13–17). Using the above Scriptures as a starting point, proclaim the Word of God over several specific areas of your life.

2. There is a direct correlation between what we are speaking out of our mouths and whether we are walking in the blessings of God. Practice speaking blessings over your life and the lives of others: blessings of rest, peace, perseverance, cheerfulness, courage, faithfulness, and prosperity.

3. Ask the Lord to show you what principalities in the spirit world are keeping you from your inheritance. As He reveals them to you, bind them, in Jesus' name!

9

Overcoming Prayerlessness

Now the Spirit speaketh expressly,
*that in the latter times **some shall depart from the faith**,*
giving heed to seducing spirits, and doctrines of devils.
—1 Timothy 4:1

*And take heed to yourselves, lest at any time your hearts be **over-***
***charged** with surfeiting, and drunkenness, and cares of this life, and*
so that day come upon you unawares.
—Luke 21:34

There is no denying that you and I are living at a very critical time. I believe we are experiencing the last days. Whether you agree with me or not, there is no dispute about the need for prayer and intercession *now* more than ever before. The poisons of secular humanism and spiritual apathy have infected many of our schools and religious institutions—including many of our churches! If we are going to experience the miraculous power of God and be His witnesses to this generation, we must become people of purposeful prayer.

Our nation's woes will not be addressed or solved by the politically focused spirit that is so prevalent today. God is not a Republican or a Democrat; He is God, and His Word is the final authority for every sincere believer in Jesus. The weapons of our warfare are not carnal or political, but mighty through God. (See 2 Corinthians 10:4.) Prayer provides the only ammunition strong enough to tear down the walls of apathy and godlessness and to bring the supernatural revival we so desperately need. Have you ever wondered why some of the most scarcely attended services are the prayer services? I believe there has been a spirit of prayerlessness released into the earth. But this is about to change! We must fight against this spirit with all our being. The good news is that you and I can overcome this spirit. Beloved, prayer should not be a chore but a wonderful encounter with the Lover of our souls. When patriotism, purity, passion, and prayer unite, our nation will see revival!

This chapter is intended to equip you with the tools you will need to overcome the spirit of prayerlessness. Jesus warned us in the gospel of Luke to "*take heed to yourselves, lest at any time your hearts be overcharged with surfeiting, and drunkenness, and cares of this life*" (Luke 21:34). The word "*overcharged*" comes from the Greek word *barynō*, which means "to weigh down." This is the only instance of this word in the entire Bible! Jesus was warning His disciples not to be weighed down with the cares, worries, and concerns of this life to the point of becoming "drunk." The truth is, it is very easy to get caught up in the "rat race" of life. That is why it is very important for us to have a deep revelation of the power and significance of prayer.

Renowned Bible teacher and author John Piper wrote, "Prayerlessness is not fundamentally a discipline problem. At root it's a faith problem."[1] Jesus was well acquainted with the temptation to focus on the natural rather than to give oneself completely to prayer. In the gospels of Matthew and Luke, we read of Jesus being led into the wilderness by the Holy Spirit to be tempted of the devil. (See Matthew 4:1–11; Luke 4:1–13.) Prayer and the Word of God were His weapons of choice for defeating the enemy; to every temptation of the devil, Jesus responded with a passage of Scripture.

Just like Jesus, we must push beyond what we think or feel and persevere in prayer. Every time we cross over the threshold of inconvenience and

1. John Piper, "Desiring God," January 23, 2015.

dare to go deeper in prayer, we open ourselves to a greater manifestation of God's presence and power.

Overcoming the Slumbering Spirit

It has been my experience that the average churchgoer finds it difficult to pray for an extended period of time. Even after just a few minutes, it seems as if either the mind begins to wander or the person becomes very sleepy. I have seen this happen frequently during sermons, as well. Have you ever wondered why some people find it extremely difficult to stay awake during a sermon, yet they become alert and vibrant as soon as the service concludes? This phenomenon is not unique to just a few people in the church; rather, it is a widespread manifestation of a very insidious ploy by the enemy of our souls.

The apostle Paul expressed this truth in the fifth chapter of Ephesians: *"Wherefore he saith, Awake* **thou that sleepest**, *and arise from the dead, and Christ shall give thee light"* (Ephesians 5:14). I believe that Paul was addressing something called the slumbering spirit. To better understand the slumbering spirit, let's take a look at Romans 11:8: *"(According as it is written, God hath given them the spirit of* **slumber**, *eyes that they should not see, and ears that they should not hear;) unto this day."* The word *"slumber"* in this verse comes from the Greek word *katanyxis,* which means "insensibility or torpor of mind." Often translated as "spirit of stupor," this condition is a state of dullness, indifference, and apathy toward spiritual things. When people are under the influence of a slumbering spirit, they are not awakened to the things of God. They are unable to pray consistently or to worship with the fervor and zeal that God desires.

You and I must understand that we were created for the purpose of being in the presence of God. As new covenant believers, we have been ordained to commune regularly with the Father in the place of prayer and intercession. Thus, it is unnatural for believers to lack a consistent prayer life. As I mentioned before, I believe that the slumbering spirit is a spiritual attack against the church. The problem is that most believers don't recognize when they are under attack. I know firsthand the struggles of being under siege by a spirit of slumber. There have been times when I didn't feel like praying at all. I assure you, this feeling originates in the pit of darkness!

A SLUMBERING SPIRIT IS A STATE OF APATHY, INDIFFERENCE, AND DULLNESS TOWARD THE THINGS OF GOD.

Just as natural sleep suspends consciousness and puts the nervous system in a state of relative inactivity, spiritual slumber suspends the prayer life of the believer. It is not all that different from sleepwalking. People who sleepwalk move around without a consciousness of their actions. If you try to speak to them while they are sleepwalking, they either do not respond or offer nonsensical replies. The same is true of many believers: God is speaking to them, but they can't hear Him because they are asleep. If you are in this condition, you need an awakening by the Holy Spirit.

Keeping the Fire Burning

The truth is that you and I have a part to play in overcoming prayerlessness in our lives. Just as a person has to exert effort to wake up in the natural, you and I have to act on the Word of God to see personal revival and awakening in our spiritual lives. Jesus admonished us in the gospel of Luke, "*Let your loins be girded about, and your lights burning*" (Luke 12:35). Prayer is analogous to a burning lamp. In Bible days, travelers carried lamps to illuminate their paths as they journeyed. There was no electricity, of course, so people had to rely on fire for light during the night. Today, prayer ignites the fire that illuminates our lives. There are specific things God wants to reveal to us that will thrust us into the blessings He has ordained for us. However, these things can be revealed only in prayer. This is why the enemy is always attempting to extinguish our prayer lives. We have to keep the fire burning!

How do we keep the fire of prayer burning in our lives? We do so first by being intentional about prayer. We must decide that prayer will be a regular part of our lives. If we don't make time for prayer, we won't pray! It is that simple.

Second, we have to meditate on the Word of God. The practices of meditating on the Word of God and praying are exponentially related: the more we read the Word, the more we will desire to pray.

Third, we must ask the Lord to create within us a hunger and a thirst for the things of God. Jesus said, *"And all things, whatsoever ye shall ask in prayer, believing, **ye shall receive**"* (Matthew 21:22). If you are certain that God will provide for your physical man, then what makes you doubt He will provide those spiritual things that you seek from Him? But don't take my word for it. Consider what Jesus said on the subject:

> *If a son shall ask bread of any of you that is a father, will he give him a stone? or if he ask a fish, will he for a fish give him a serpent? Or if he shall ask an egg, will he offer him a scorpion? If ye then, being evil, know how to give good gifts unto your children: how much more shall your heavenly Father give the Holy Spirit to them that ask him?*
>
> (Luke 11:11–13)

I declare that the Holy Spirit is igniting a flame in your spirit that will cause you to desire the things of God more than ever before. As we navigate through perilous times, we must be fully engaged in prophetic prayer and intercession.

I will never forget the time I experienced a forest fire. Unfortunately, I was the one who caused it! One hot summer day, I was playing in the woods with another kid from our neighborhood. We took a lighter and ignited some dry straw on the ground. Before we knew it, the fire had spread to a larger area; and it continued to grow, despite our best attempts to put it out. At that point, we did the only thing we knew to do: we ran! By God's grace, someone called the fire department; but, by the time a truck arrived, significant damage had been done. Nearly burning down a local forest at least taught me a valuable lesson: once a fire gets started, it is very difficult to stop. That's why the enemy's greatest fear is a church on fire for God. It is time for the church to wake up! It is time for all believers to arise! We must be set ablaze by the supernatural fire of the Holy Spirit, who never sleeps. When this happens, prayer will no longer be a duty; it will become a delight. God is waiting on us to fuel the fires of prayer with the Word of God, worship, and thanksgiving. This is the key to experiencing supernatural breakthrough!

The Mystery of the Ten Virgins

In the gospel of Matthew, Jesus shares a powerful parable that masterfully illustrates the necessity of remaining vigilant in prayer.

> *Then shall the kingdom of heaven be likened unto ten virgins, which took their lamps, and went forth to meet the bridegroom. And five of them were wise, and five were foolish. They that were foolish took their lamps, and took no oil with them: but the wise took oil in their vessels with their lamps. While the bridegroom tarried, they all slumbered and slept. And at midnight there was a cry made, Behold, the bridegroom cometh; go ye out to meet him. Then all those virgins arose, and trimmed their lamps. And the foolish said unto the wise, Give us of your oil; for our lamps are gone out. But the wise answered, saying, Not so; lest there be not enough for us and you: but go ye rather to them that sell, and buy for yourselves. And while they went to buy, the bridegroom came; and they that were ready went in with him to the marriage: and the door was shut. Afterward came also the other virgins, saying, Lord, Lord, open to us. But he answered and said, Verily I say unto you, I know you not. Watch therefore, for ye know neither the day nor the hour wherein the Son of man cometh.*   (Matthew 25:1–13)

This parable should be a powerful warning for the church today. The virgins who failed to bring additional oil for their lamps were called "*foolish.*" The Greek word has an even deeper meaning: "impious or godless," which implies a lack of respect or reverence for God. Most Christians would never consider themselves irreverent or godless; and yet, when it comes to prayer, they don't invest much time, if any, in doing it. The foolish virgins were unwilling to invest in oil for their lamps. In Scripture, oil is often used to symbolize the anointing of the Holy Spirit; but in this particular passage, the oil represents literal fuel. Putting oil in one's lamp is an act of intentionality that represents a deliberate act of faith and obedience on the part of the believer. Prayer is the "oil" with which we fuel our spiritual lives, that we might be ready for whatever the Lord sends our way. Remember, nothing catches a praying person by surprise!

> PRAYER PREPARES US FOR OUR TIME OF VISITATION. THE MORE TIME WE SPEND IN PRAYER, THE MORE PREPARED WE BECOME.

The parable of the ten virgins is typically viewed as an illustration of the end times. While this is valid, I believe that the passage also bears relevance to the present life of every believer. Notice that all ten virgins—wise and foolish alike—were asleep until they heard the clarion call of the bridegroom, at which point they arose and went to meet Him. The difference was that the five foolish virgins realized their lamps had run out of oil, and asked to borrow oil from the other five virgins. Because the foolish virgins had no oil, what should have been their time of visitation became a time of preparation—and they didn't receive entrance to the Lord's presence.

God wants to meet with us in the place of prayer and intercession. But we cannot "borrow oil" from anyone else, because our devotion to God and intimacy with Him are personal. Yes, it is possible to pray for others and to see corresponding change in their lives; but nothing can take the place of personal devotion. Your pastor's prayer life has nothing to do with your prayer life. You must have intimacy with God for yourself.

The Three Dimensions of Prayer

One of the biggest problems in the church when it comes to prayer is that the average believer doesn't really know what prayer is. Those who have engaged in genuine prayer to some degree can testify that prayer is an extremely powerful activity. However, many people have yet to see the fullness of what God intended them to experience in prayer. What if there were more to prayer—so much more—than what we have experienced?

There was a season in my life when I sought God as never before. He would wake me up in the middle of the night for months on end, giving me the impression that He wanted to talk with me. It was during this season that I had several of my first miraculous encounters with God, and I realized that there was much more to prayer than I had experienced to that point. As I sought the Lord with all my heart, miracles began to manifest in my life. Prayer is the bedrock of the supernatural!

I believe that there are three dimensions to prayer. When you understand this revelation, it will change the way you pray for the rest of your life. God instructed Moses, *"And let them make me a sanctuary; that I may dwell among them. According to all that I shew thee, after the pattern of the tabernacle, and the pattern of all the instruments thereof, even so shall ye make it"* (Exodus 25:8–9). The pattern of the tabernacle in the wilderness is a prophetic picture of the New Testament believer because, according to 1 Corinthians 6:19, our bodies are the temple (or tabernacle) of the Holy Spirit.

God told Moses to build the temple *"according to...the pattern."* The word here for *"pattern," tabniyth,* means "plan, form, construction, or figure." What God told Moses about the tabernacle in the wilderness also applies to us today, because it is a prophetic picture. Each of us must ask ourselves, *Am I following the rules for prayer?* The reason why many people are not experiencing the supernatural in prayer is because they are not praying according to God's divine pattern. The three dimensions of prayer correspond to the three dimensions of the tabernacle in the Old Testament: the outer court, the inner court (or Holy Place), and the Holy of Holies.

The outer-court dimension

In the Old Testament tabernacle, the outer court was the place where the common Israelites congregated. In other words, this was the common place. Most people can identify with this aspect of prayer because it is a common part of religious experience. It represents the natural, or fleshly, realm—the place where we approach God with thanksgiving for the things He has done and the gifts He has given us. The outer court is based on what we can see, sense, and feel in the natural world. This is the physical dimension of prayer.

The problem with the outer court is that it is based on the natural realm—the things we can see with our physical eyes. "Outer-court" prayer is a very limited form of prayer, for much of what God does in our lives begins in the invisible realm.

In the Old Testament tabernacle, the outer court contained the brazen laver, which the priests would use for ceremonial handwashing in preparation for ministry. In the same way, the outer-court dimension of prayer is a place of preparation, where God prepares our hearts to go deeper. Unfortunately, most believers never move beyond the outer-court experience into the Holy Place (or inner court). Many people never get the opportunity to experience God beyond the limitations of their flesh and their emotions. In order to go deeper than the outer court, we must move beyond emotion-based prayer and tap into the Spirit of God. Even if we don't feel anything, we should keep praying until we reach a deeper level!

The inner-court dimension

The second dimension of prayer is the inner court. Within the inner court of the tabernacle were three elements: the candlestick, the showbread, and the altar of incense. These elements represented sacrifices to the Lord. I believe that these elements also represent different aspects of the prayer life of a born-again believer under the new covenant. The candlestick, or menorah, represents the believer. Jesus made several allusions to the candlestick in reference to His disciples, including this one from the gospel of Matthew:

> Ye are the light of the world. A city that is set on an hill cannot be hid. Neither do men light a candle, and put it under a bushel, but on a candlestick; and it giveth light unto all that are in the house. Let your light so shine before men, that they may see your good works, and glorify your Father which is in heaven. (Matthew 5:14–16)

We are the menorah of the Lord, which is to blaze continually for His glory. We cannot be a light to the world unless our candle has been lit in prayer! Inside the inner court, things are burned and consumed. When we move into the inner-court dimension of prayer, we encounter the fire of God, and anything that is not of the nature of Jesus is burned out of us. The fire of God ignites us from within and brings revelation to every area of our lives. Remember, candlesticks were designed to be set on fire.

Also in the inner court was the showbread (or shewbread), which comes from the Hebrew word *lechem*, meaning "bread of the presence." Many scholars believe that it was thus named because of the command to keep the showbread before the Lord continually. (See, for example, Leviticus 24:8.) I believe that the showbread represents the unleavened heart of the believer and the constant remembrance of the Passover from Egypt. It is in the inner court that we recall the instances of God's faithfulness toward us. The inner court is a place of testimony. The root word for "showbread," *lâcham*, actually means to fight, do battle, or make war. Sometimes, you and I have to battle in order to remember all the good that God has done amid the trials we have faced (and even may be currently facing). This is spiritual warfare!

THE INNER COURT IS A PLACE WHERE THE BELIEVER GAINS VICTORY IN SPIRITUAL BATTLE!

Finally, there is the altar of incense, which was to burn continually within the Holy Place. The altar of incense is a prophetic symbol of constant praise and thanksgiving, which is why the writer of Hebrews would later say, *"By him therefore let us offer the sacrifice of praise to God continually, that is, the fruit of our lips giving thanks to his name"* (Hebrews 13:15). Praise and thanksgiving are just as much a part of prayer as intercession or supplication. In fact, praise and thanksgiving are prophetic activities because they are not based upon our feelings or our circumstances. The more we give thanks, in faith, and praise God in spite of our circumstances, the more we see the manifestation of His power in our lives.

The Holy-of-Holies dimension

The Holy of Holies (or Most Holy Place) is the area in the tabernacle beyond the veil; it could be accessed by the high priest alone, just once a year. The significance of the Holy of Holies is that it housed the ark of the covenant, representing the manifest presence of God. I believe that there is a place in prayer (beyond the veil) where you and I can encounter the manifest presence of God. I call this place the "Glory Zone." It is here that eternity literally invades the atmosphere, and time stands still. When we have entered into the Holy of Holies through prayer, time is no longer a factor.

Once, when I was praying, it was almost as if I was in another dimension because I was no longer conscious of time. When I came out of the prayer, I looked at the clock and realized that I had been praying for three hours, but it felt like three minutes. Through the blood of Jesus, every born-again believer can access the Holy-of-Holies dimension of prayer.

We must be willing to make the necessary sacrifice to experience the glory of God—and the sacrifice is the abandonment of self! Are you willing to lose yourself in prayer? Are you willing to be more than just an "outer-court" believer? It is time for the church to graduate beyond the outer- and inner-court experiences and to enter into the Glory Zone. Whenever the glory of God is made manifest, the power of heaven is revealed. Can you imagine your entire list of prayer requests being answered in a moment? Can you imagine God using you as a prophetic intercessor to shake the nations through prayer? There is far more to prayer than asking God to heal your body, restore your finances, or deliver your loved ones. Through prayer, we have access to heaven on earth.

Are You a Fair-weather Believer?

Do you know someone who is always making excuses and failing to keep his or her commitments when it is not convenient to do so? Do you have a friend or loved one that always tells you, "We are going to have lunch one day!" yet it has been three years and you haven't had lunch yet? Have you met anyone who refuses to go somewhere because the weather is bad? Many believers are the very same way with their prayer lives, basing their devotion and obedience to God on external circumstances. I call these people "fair-weather believers." They only come to church when they "feel like it." They only give tithes and offerings when it is convenient for them, and they rarely step out of their comfort zones. Fair-weather believers always complain that they are not seeing God move in their lives, yet they refuse to make the sacrifice necessary to experience the presence of God. Worst of all, many fair-weather believers invoke the grace of God to justify their spiritual laziness and apathy.

Beloved, we must not be among those who make excuses. We must be willing to step out in faith, even when it is storming all around us. Proverbs 26:13 gives us a picture of someone who makes excuses: "*The **slothful** man saith, There is a lion in the way; a lion is in the streets.*" The word "*slothful*" here means sluggish or lazy. Spiritual laziness is like cancer; it usually starts out small, but, if left untreated, it can spread throughout the entire body. We cannot afford to be spiritually lazy. What if I told you that every seed we sow in prayer produces a harvest? How would your approach to prayer change? What if I told you that every word proceeding out of our mouths in prayer will come to pass? Well, that is exactly what is going to happen! Jesus said, "*What things soever ye desire, when ye pray, **believe that ye receive them, and ye shall have them**"* (Mark 11:24).

Praying in the Holy Spirit

One of the most neglected aspects of prayer in the church today is praying in the Holy Spirit. The Word of God admonishes us to pray without ceasing. (See 1 Thessalonians 5:17.) How can we fulfill this mandate? I believe that the only way you and I can be obedient to the Word of God in this area is to develop the habit of praying in the Holy Spirit.

In 1906, a man by the name of William J. Seymour began to preach on the baptism of the Holy Spirit with the evidence of speaking in other tongues. Ironically, some sources say that, at the time, he had yet to experience this phenomenon himself. Eventually, he received the gift of tongues, and thus began the famous Azusa Street Revival. I believe this was a critical time in the body of Christ because the revelation of the baptism in the Holy Spirit caused a dramatic shift in the framework of the church. As more and more people caught this revelation, notable miracles broke out. Hallelujah!

I am grateful for the heritage of the Holy Spirit in the United States, but I believe it is time for a resurgence—not just of the gift of tongues but also of an awareness of the power of praying in the Holy Spirit. Unfortunately, many charismatic and Pentecostal churches do not make a regular practice of praying in the Spirit. The apostle Paul said, *"For if I pray in an **unknown tongue**, my spirit prayeth"* (1 Corinthians 14:14). Did you know that when you pray in tongues your spirit man is praying? I have personally benefited from the power of praying in the Spirit. Oftentimes, when I am praying for someone, I will take a few minutes to pray in tongues for that person. When I do this, a very powerful thing occurs: the Holy Spirit downloads words of wisdom and words of knowledge into my spirit for that individual.

PRAYING IN TONGUES IS LIKE PLUGGING INTO A NUCLEAR REACTOR. THE HOLY SPIRIT FILLS OUR SOULS WITH MIRACLE POWER!

There are many benefits of praying in tongues. First of all, the act of praying in tongues bypasses our minds and emotions, enabling us to tap into our spirit man. (See 1 Corinthians 14:14.) Second, praying in tongues gives us access to the mysteries of God. And, third, when we pray in the Holy Spirit, we pray directly to God, transcending the limits of our human understanding. (See 1 Corinthians 14:2.) Praying in the Holy Spirit builds up the believer on his or her faith. (See Jude 1:20.)

Prophetic Prayer

Right now, in the precious name of Jesus and through the eternal power of His blood, I take authority over the spirits of witchcraft, manipulation, deception, control, and bitterness. I command all word curses, whether spoken over myself or believed by me, to be broken, in Jesus' name. All spirits of deception, seduction, and lying are broken and released from their ungodly assignments in my life and/or the lives of those around me. All physical infirmities or mind-binding attacks associated with witchcraft are canceled, broken, defeated, and destroyed by the power of the blood of Jesus. All instances of autoimmune disease, cancerous growth, chronic pain, mental illness, emotional bondage, and confusion are broken, once and for all, in Jesus' mighty name! Amen.

Prophetic Insights

1. What was Jesus' weapon of choice for fighting the devil? (See Matthew 4:1–11; Luke 4:1–13.)

2. What are the three ways to keep the fire of prayer burning in your life?

3. What are the three dimensions of prayer identified in this chapter? Have you accessed all three in your prayers?

10

Becoming a World Changer

*Now then we are **ambassadors** for Christ, as though God did beseech you by us: we pray you in Christ's stead, be ye reconciled to God.*
—2 Corinthians 5:20

Earlier, we explored the concept of being ambassadors for Christ, specifically as intercessors. This concept is so important, it is worth exploring in greater detail.

The Bible calls us *"ambassadors for Christ."* What does this mean? Simply put, you and I are Christ's representatives in the earth. As such, we have the responsibility to "colonize" the earth, to the extent that it begins to look like heaven. Please don't get me wrong—I don't believe the Bible encourages us to create a pseudo-utopian society where everyone walks around barefoot and sings worship songs while playing the acoustic guitar. But I do believe we have the power and responsibility to bring change to the world around us for the glory of God.

The word *"ambassadors"* in 2 Corinthians 5:20 comes from the Greek root *presbyteros*, which means "those who...managed public affairs and administered justice." Remember, we established that prayer has to do with justice and vindication. We have been given the charge and the authority to become "world changers": those who administer justice (in a spiritual sense) in the affairs of the earth.

One day, my wife and I received a prayer request from a family member on behalf of a coworker who had been kidnapped and held for ransom. Apparently, the kidnappers were so vicious, they cut off one of the victim's fingers and sent it to his family. It was a horrifying situation, to say the least! My wife and I began to pray for this person, declaring that the kidnappers would release him unharmed, in Jesus' name. I'm sure that we weren't the only ones who were praying! We also asked God to manifest His justice in the situation. A few days later, the man was released from captivity, safe and sound. Hallelujah! What if my wife and I had been too busy to pray? What if no one had had the audacity to ask for God's divine intervention? This is why it is critical that we embrace our calling as prophetic prayer warriors and ambassadors.

OUR SPIRITUAL AMBASSADORSHIP EXTENDS BEYOND OUR NATURAL VOCATION AND OUR SOCIAL STATUS.

The purpose of revival and awakening is not to experience a fuzzy feeling in one's stomach but to be empowered to bring change to the world. For too long, the church has acted as a spiritual thermometer rather than a spiritual thermostat. We have allowed the popular culture to determine our "temperature"—and to cool our spiritual zeal—rather than acting as the pacesetters God has called us to be. A thermostat has the power to alter the atmosphere it controls. As prophetic intercessors, we have the power to transform the atmosphere around us. But before we can become agents of change, we must first undergo change and transformation in our personal lives. This change begins by our accepting who God says we are. No longer must we be people to whom life just "happens."

Occupy Until He Comes

I am an ardent believer that we are in the end-times. The signs all around us point to the truth that Jesus is coming back sooner than most people think. But some individuals have gone as far as to calculate the date and time of His coming, even though the Scriptures assure us that no one knows when He will return. (See, for example, Matthew 24:36.) Other individuals who share my belief that we are living in the end times have now have embraced a "doom and gloom" theology that they believe exempts them from any responsibility regarding the condition of the world they live in. Some of them have become so obsessed with calamity that every natural disaster or tragedy becomes a justification for their cynicism masked as religious piety. Beloved, I don't believe either of these extreme philosophies is biblical.

Jesus expresses a much different perspective in this parable, recorded in the gospel of Luke:

> A certain nobleman went into a far country to receive for himself a kingdom, and to return. And he called his ten servants, and delivered them ten pounds, and said unto them, Occupy till I come.
>
> (Luke 19:12–13)

The term "occupy" in this passage comes from the Greek word *pragmateuomai*, which means "to carry on a business." In other words, Jesus told His disciples to carry on the Father's business until His return.

Imagine that a father who owns a business has to go away on an important trip, so he puts his son in charge during his absence. Do you think the son will fail to show up at work? Do you think he will allow the books to go unbalanced or the employees to stay home all day? God forbid! Why, then, do many people think that they are to simply hide at home and look for Jesus to crack the sky? The Lord wants believers to be about His business of advancing the kingdom, one soul at a time, one act of obedience at a time.

God wants us to pray about the things going on in our world. He wants us to be sentinels and watchmen on the wall, interceding on behalf of those around us. He wants us to be His agents in the earth. And we can't do that if we are apathetic toward spiritual things.

In 2011, a movement in the United States known as Occupy Wall Street rocked the national consciousness with its cry against social and economic inequality. Using large-scale protests, sit-ins, and other forms of civil disobedience, the protesters literally "shut down" Wall Street to the point of affecting the business operations of some of the major banks and investment companies in the area. The movement gained international attention as it expanded beyond Wall Street to university campuses, board meetings, and foreclosed homes. The protests were designed to disrupt "business as usual."

I would argue that it is time for the church to "Occupy Earth." Through prayer and intercession, we can disrupt "business as usual." I am all for voting and passing legislation, but I think it is time for us to start legislating from inside our prayer closets, as well. We can storm the heavens with prayer and demand to see change and transformation in our schools, businesses, churches, communities, and cities. We will never operate in the ambassadorial anointing Jesus has given us if we don't accept the truth that we are to be more than just silent pew-warmers. The Father has left the church in charge and has empowered her to fulfill this divine assignment.

Supernatural Transformation

The apostle Paul exhorts us in Romans 12:2, *"And be not conformed to this world: but be ye transformed by the renewing of your mind, that ye may prove what is that good, and acceptable, and perfect, will of God."* The word *"transformed"* in this verse comes from the Greek word *metamorphoō*, from which we get the word *metamorphosis*—the term for the transformation of a caterpillar into a butterfly, for example. Before a caterpillar knows what it feels like to fly, it first must undergo a metamorphosis, or a complete change of form or nature.

When we became born again, we underwent a supernatural metamorphosis. God changed us from sinners into saints, from unrighteous to righteous. However, there is another transformation that you and I must undergo. We must also be transformed into agents of change—individuals who can be strategically used in the hand of God to make a difference in our particular sphere of influence. No matter where you are, you can be an agent of change on your job, in your church, or in your school. God is waiting on you to step out in faith and to come into agreement with His word for your life.

What does this have to do with prayer? Everything! Through prayer, we release the ambassadorial authority that Christ has given us. Through prayer, we bring about positive change in people's lives. We may be the only picture of Christ that someone else sees. It is time for us to prove to the world around us that the will of God is good, acceptable, and perfect, as Romans 12:2 says it is. And the only way to do that is to pray for the world rather than to condemn it.

In the realm of foreign affairs, every ambassador is given control over a specific territory, usually referred to as an embassy. And every embassy is meant to look exactly like the country it represents. A woman who had visited the embassy of a Middle Eastern country described to me how posh the embassy was in terms of amenities and décor. It was no surprise to me, considering the particular country the ambassadors were representing is very wealthy. It is only fitting that the embassy convey the nation's wealth and opulence.

When Christ was on earth, He was an Ambassador whose embassy conveyed the glory of the "country" that He came from.

> *And after six days Jesus taketh with him Peter, and James, and John, and leadeth them up into an high mountain apart by themselves: and he was transfigured before them. And his raiment became shining, exceeding white as snow; so as no fuller on earth can white them.*
>
> (Mark 9:2–3)

For many years, I assumed that this passage of Scripture was just an instance of Jesus showing His divinity to the disciples. But then, I began to wonder: What if He had another purpose for this transfiguration? What if Jesus was giving His disciples a glimpse of what happened whenever He went to pray? I don't believe that the act of transfiguration was a rare occurrence for Jesus. We know that He was God, but we also know He was a man, anointed by the power of the Holy Spirit. He simply invited the disciples into the "embassy" of heaven while they were on the mountain with Him.

THROUGH PRAYER, BELIEVERS CAN RELEASE THE
EMBASSY OF GOD ON THE EARTH.

When the purpose, power, and presence of God convene, heaven invades the earth. If we are people of prayer, then everywhere we go can become a heavenly embassy. I challenge you to go and colonize your neighborhood through prayer. I promise you that things will never look the same again. In a sense, we must undergo a transfiguration of our own.

More than Mortal

I often hear people say, "But, Pastor, I am only human!" Perhaps that is what you are thinking right now: *This all sound goods, but I'm just human!* Although I understand the attitude from which this statement is spoken, I can say with confidence that it is not compatible with a biblical perspective. If we have the Holy Spirit living on the inside of us, then we are not just mere mortal men and women. The Bible tells us, *"Therefore if any man be in Christ, he is a **new creature**: old things are passed away; behold, all things are become **new**"* (2 Corinthians 5:17).

According to this passage, you and I are brand-new creations in Christ. We are a new species, as it were, created in the image of Jesus. We are more than mere men and women—we are supernatural beings, endowed with power, authority, and dominion. Simply put, we are Jesus people! When you recognize that you are a Jesus person, you can begin to change the world around you. Why? The Bible says, *"Ye are of God, little children, and have overcome them: because **greater is he that is in you, than he that is in the world**"* (1 John 4:4). Did you know that the One who lives in you is greater than the system of this world? Too often, we adopt the mentality of a powerless victim. This is nothing but a ploy of the enemy to keep us from being the people of power and influence that God has called us to be. That's right—you are a person of great power and influence! In fact, the Holy Spirit on the inside of you is *infectious*.

> ## WE HAVE BEEN CALLED BY GOD TO BE PEOPLE OF SUPERNATURAL POWER AND INFLUENCE IN THE EARTH.

Prayer is all about exerting our kingdom influence on the situations and circumstances around us. Have you ever been in a situation that seemed absolutely chaotic? Have you ever been overwhelmed by trials and temptations? If so, I have good news for you: greater is the One who lives in you than he that is in the world. (See 1 John 4:4.) Your trials and difficulties can't break you, because the Spirit inside of you is unbreakable. Instead of giving in to the chaos and confusion around you, set your shoulders and declare, "Let there be light!" Remember, light is more powerful than darkness. You must recognize that the kingdom of God within you is stronger than anything else. Whether you are praying for your family members to come to salvation or for a loved one to be healed of a physical ailment, you are not "just human," because you are a child of God. Prayer has the power to alter the fabric of your situation, but you have to release your faith as you pray without ceasing.

Let Your Light Shine!

Many years ago, soon after I was born again, there weren't many young people serving the Lord the way I was. It was very difficult for me as a Spirit-filled, teenage believer; I realized firsthand that being a Christian could be a lonely walk. I was faced with a critical choice: either conform to my environment or become an influencer of my environment. I believe that God allows a certain level of isolation (and sometimes persecution) in our lives, to challenge us to overcome the pressures around us. Jesus said, "*Let your light so shine before men, that they may see your good works, and glorify your Father which is in heaven*" (Matthew 5:16). I began to meditate on the Word of God and pray like there was no tomorrow. I would wake up at five every morning and pray until it was time to go to school. Something phenomenal began to take place. People started to see the change in my life. They would say to me, "What is going on with you? Something is different about you!" I didn't know it, but Matthew 5:16 was coming to fruition in my life. I was allowing the light of Christ to shine through me.

You have the same light on the inside of you; now is the time to let it shine! In the world, there's something I like to call the Law of Environment, which claims that your environment will influence you before you influence your environment. While this may be true in the natural sense, it is not true of the born-again believer. Light is greater than darkness; therefore, you have the ability to penetrate the darkness in whatever environment you find yourself in. This isn't a license for believers to spend their time hanging around bars and pubs, but it does mean that you have the ability to manifest the kingdom of God wherever you go. Notice that the key to my light shining was a consistent prayer life. If we are not praying, we are not influencing.

THE KEY TO BEING A KINGDOM INFLUENCER IS PRAYER. PRAYER ENABLES US TO OVERPOWER OUR ENVIRONMENT.

In my years of ministry, I have counseled thousands of people who complained of being persecuted by their family members. Many of them were young people still living at home. They would often say something along the lines of, "Pastor, you don't understand my family dynamics!" The truth is, your family dynamics are irrelevant. It is your internal dynamics that is more important. What is going on inside of us?

Fans of science fiction are probably familiar with terraforming, or the hypothetical process of transforming another planet to resemble the earth, especially for the purpose of making it capable of supporting human life. In a way, you and I have the power to "heaven-form" our environment, transforming it so that it looks more like heaven. Through prayer, we can change the atmosphere of our home or place of employment. We must simply pray, "Father, I thank You that this house or workplace is conducive to the working of your Holy Spirit. I declare that anything operating in this environment that is not like You must leave right now, in the name of Jesus. I release the presence of God to fill the atmosphere right now."

If we pray like this on a consistent basis, we will begin to see positive change take place. Remember, when God wants to bring order to chaos, He always speaks to the atmosphere. We must do the same!

All Things Are Possible

One of my favorite movies is *Mission Impossible*, starring Tom Cruise. In this spin-off of the original television series from the 1960s, Tom Cruise plays a member of the IMF (Impossible Mission Force), whose constituents are responsible for solving the most difficult problems in government and geopolitical affairs. They are called in only when the situation is impossible. Oftentimes, they save the world without anyone knowing who they are. No matter how difficult the task, the IMF always gets the job done.

You and I are part of an Impossible Mission Force: the kingdom of God! Jesus said, "*With men this is impossible; but with God **all things are possible**" (Matthew 19:26). No matter how impossible the situations in your life may seem, you can overcome them because you possess the overcomers' anointing. If God has placed you in a difficult family, in a challenging job, or among the unlikeliest people, it is because He has commissioned you as a supernatural agent of change. You have the supernatural equipment to get the job done.

Unlike the characters in the fictional movie, the weapons and technology that we use are not carnal or natural, but spiritual. (See 2 Corinthians 10:4.) Every time we pray, we are using our supernatural weapons to overcome the impossible. Whatever we need for the mission is available to us in prayer. All we have to do is call on the name of Jesus. The Bible says we can do all things through Christ who strengthens us. (See Philippians 4:13.) Prayer opens our spirit man to the endless possibilities of God.

I don't care what you are going through; there is always a solution. There is always an answer, and there is always a way out! So, I charge you today to go forward in faith, knowing that all things are possible if you simply believe. Your mission, if you choose to accept it, is to change your community, church, school, home, and family. Are you up for the challenge? Are you ready to do the impossible and experience the supernatural? What are you waiting for?

Prophetic Prayer

Father, in the name of Jesus, I thank You for who You are and for all You have done in my life. I declare that I am holy, as You are holy. I walk in holiness. Right now, in Jesus' name, I consecrate myself through Your Word, and I declare that I am sanctified through Your truth. I am not the same as the world, but I am set apart from the world. People will look at me and know that I am a child of God. The DNA of God the Father fills my very being right now. I am filled with the fullness of God today. I am part of a chosen generation, a royal priesthood, a peculiar people, a holy nation; and today, I praise You because You have called me out of darkness into Your marvelous light, Lord. I separate myself from all that is unclean, including sinful desires, thoughts, emotions, and actions. I walk in purity, both bodily and in my mind. In Jesus' name, amen!

Prophetic Insights

1. What is the church's divine assignment, to be performed until Christ comes again?

2. Are believers "mere mortals"?

3. How can you "heaven-form" the world around you?

PROPHETIC PRACTICUM

1. Do you have a slumbering spirit? Rebuke it in the name of Jesus, and wake to the power of glory of the Holy Spirit.

2. Over the next few days, pay attention to the frequency with which your mouth makes excuses, remembering that it's often the slumbering, slothful spirit that prompts excuses.

3. Through prayer and intercession, we can disrupt "business as usual." What are some social issues or injustices that are close to your heart? "Legislate from the prayer closet" by proclaiming God's power over them.

4. When God wants to bring order from chaos, He always speaks to the atmosphere. Today, speak into the atmospheres of chaos that you see around you in your workplace, your community, your home, or wherever you happen to be.

11

Prayer: The Greater Work

*Verily, verily, I say unto you, He that believeth on me, the works that
I do shall he do also; and greater works than these shall he do; because
I go unto my Father.*
—John 14:12

In the fourteenth chapter of John, Jesus admonishes His disciples to believe on Him, and explains to them that whoever believes will do the things He did—and even greater things. (See John 14:12.) This statement is one of the most powerful and controversial Scriptures in the Bible. Religion and tradition have taught us that we are nothing like Jesus. In most traditional churches, the preacher would have a heart attack if you told him you could do the same things Jesus did. Yet this is exactly what the Bible says.

The question remains: what did Jesus mean by *"greater works"*? We know that He healed the sick, cleansed the lepers, and raised the dead; so, what kinds of miracles qualify as "greater works"? The answer to this question is, I believe, simpler than we might think. It is found in John 14:13: *"And whatsoever ye shall ask in my name, that will I do, that the Father may be glorified in the Son."* Have you ever considered that prayer might be the greater work? Through prayer, we have unlimited access to the Father. We can ask anything in the Father's name, and it will be done. Do you really believe this?

If we recognized prayer as the "greater work," we would probably do more praying. I am not suggesting that God expects us to spend ten hours in prayer every day, but I am saying that prayer should be a priority in our lives. Before Jesus died on the cross and arose again, the disciples had to rely on Him to secure whatever they needed from God. After His resurrection, Jesus gave the disciples—and all believers throughout the ages, ourselves included—the right to use His name to approach the Father directly. In essence, we have received the unlimited power of Jesus. This is the reason we can lay hands on the sick and see them recover. This is also the reason we can live in the miraculous every day. It is time for us to stop arguing with God and to be about the Father's business!

I would like to ask again an important question I posed earlier: What would happen if we believed with all our heart that every word spoken in prayer would come to pass? How would it change the way we pray? Would we still murmur and complain? Would we still worry?

UNDER THE NEW COVENANT, WE HAVE THE SAME ACCESS TO MIRACLES, SIGNS, AND WONDERS AS JESUS—THE SAME, AND EVEN GREATER!

Have you ever considered the fact that you have an audience with the very Creator of the universe? Have you thought about how blessed you are to be able to commune with the One who set the sun in the sky? Prayer is, by definition, a supernatural activity. Every time we pray in faith, something changes. The more we meditate on this truth, the more it will change our lives. The Bible says, *"How God anointed Jesus of Nazareth with the Holy Spirit and with power: who went about doing good, and healing all that were oppressed of the devil; for God was with him"* (Acts 10:38). Notice that Jesus Christ went about manifesting the kingdom of God. Everything He did was an outflow from His prayer life. He had an inextricable connection with the Father. And you and I can have that same connection, today and for all eternity.

Communion with the Father

We must never underestimate the privilege of keeping unbroken communion with the Father through prayer. Jesus said, *"If a man love me, he will keep my words: and my Father will love him, and we will come unto him, and make our abode with him"* (John 14:23). The word *"abode"* in this verse comes from the Greek word *monē*, which means "a staying, abiding, dwelling." It is a metaphoric picture of the Holy Spirit indwelling believers. In the Bible days, abiding with someone signified friendship and communion. It was not customary to abide in the house of your enemies; this type of fellowship was reserved for those who shared deep intimacy with one another. Through the Holy Spirit, we have the "abiding" kind of communion and deep intimacy with God.

Before we were born again, we were estranged from God; because of our sinful nature, we could not fellowship with Him. In the Old Testament, the high priest was permitted to enter the Holy of Holies just once a year—a poignant illustration of this truth. But under the new covenant, we have a permanent seat in Holy of Holies. Communion is the sharing or exchanging of intimate thoughts and feelings, especially on a mental or spiritual level. The Father wants to exchange thoughts with us in prayer. Can you imagine? This is why Jesus was always in a position to perform miracles. The Bible records Him as saying, *"The Son can do nothing of himself, but what he seeth the Father do: for what things soever he doeth, these also doeth the Son likewise"* (John 5:19). Everything that Jesus did was born out of communion with the Father. Again, He said, *"The Son can do nothing of himself."* If you desire to experience the miraculous in your life, you must first come to the realization that you can do nothing of yourself. We must learn to rely on God.

PRAYER IS A DEMONSTRATION OF OUR COMPLETE RELIANCE ON GOD AND HIS POWER IN EVERY AREA OF OUR LIVES.

When we are in communion with God, we have confidence that He will answer us whenever we call on Him. The Bible declares, *"And this is the **confidence** that we have in him, that, if we ask any thing according to his will, **he heareth us**"* (1 John 5:14). One time, I was praying for a woman to be healed of paralysis. In the natural world, there was no solution to her problem; but I was sure God would have the final say. I knew with all my heart that it was the perfect will of God for her to be healed, not only because the Word declares it (see, for example, 1 Peter 2:24), but also because the Lord had revealed it to me. (Often God wants to reveal His heart and mind to us so that we can manifest His will in the earth.) I prayed over this woman in faith, believing for a miracle. Even when it seemed nothing had changed, I continued praying for her. Finally, something broke off of her, spiritually, and she received her healing in a matter of minutes. This was the greater work in action! Just as Jesus did what He saw the Father doing (see John 5:19), you and I can do what we see the Father doing—on a regular basis. We have to train ourselves to live this way. We must spend time in prayer so that we can develop the spiritual sensitivity that is necessary to walk in the miraculous. Isn't it amazing that everywhere Jesus went, something supernatural happened? I declare that everywhere you go, something supernatural will occur.

The Mystery of the Prayer Closet

Jesus gave us specific directions on how to pray:

> *But thou, when thou prayest, enter into thy **closet**, and when thou hast shut thy door, pray to thy Father which is in secret; and thy Father which seeth in secret shall reward thee openly.* (Matthew 6:6)

What does it mean to enter into your closet and shut the door? The Greek word for *"closet"* in this verse indicates a storeroom or a secret chamber. Just as a bride and her bridegroom consummate their marriage vows in a secret chamber, so too you and I have been invited to commune with the Father in the secret place.

The secret place of prayer is a place of intimacy and disclosure. The Bible says, *"He that dwelleth in the **secret place** of the most High shall abide under the shadow of the Almighty"* (Psalm 91:1). Our prayer closet is not a physical place limited by location and availability; it is a relationship we have with God that we can access twenty-four hours a day.

During the time of Christ, rabbinical leaders would wear a vestment called a tallit, or prayer shawl, that symbolized the tent of meeting in the Old Testament. This shawl, or tallit, was an integral part of Jewish prayer customs in the first century. Even in modern times, Jewish men wear a tallit when praying at the Western Wall in Jerusalem. The idea is that in wearing the shawl, they carry the tent of meeting with them wherever they go, because it is portable and accessible. In the same way, you and I have an unlimited invitation to enter the secret place and bring our petitions before God. Most believers don't understand the deep spiritual significance of this invitation, which is probably why they don't make an investment in their prayer lives. We commune with God in secret so that we may manifest the fruit of the secret place openly. Just as the fruit of the intimacy between a husband and wife is born nine months later, the fruit of our prayer lives will always manifest openly at some point.

EVERY SEED SOWN IN THE SECRET PLACE OF PRAYER WILL PRODUCE A VISIBLE HARVEST FOR ALL TO SEE.

As I mentioned earlier, when I first became a believer, God led me into a season of intense prayer. The more I prayed, the more amazing results I saw in my life. I began to walk in the supernatural, and I received words of knowledge and wisdom on a regular basis. Embracing the discipline of prayer caused me to come into alignment with the will and purposes of God. Some people around me attributed this phenomenon to over-the-top zeal and enthusiasm, but I believe that this type of experience is meant to be a sustainable part of our Christian lives. God is eager to reveal to you His mind concerning the various areas of your life. He wants to show you the things that will shortly come to pass.

One day, I was praying about a challenging situation I was going through, and the Holy Spirit began to disclose some key facts to me. I was amazed as I saw that nothing was as it had seemed to be. I wonder how many areas of our lives could benefit from a Holy Spirit "reality check." How many times have we misjudged people and situations because we neglected to pray about them? Prayer is the ethos of the Christian life; without it, we cannot stay connected to the realm of the spirit. However, when we embrace prayer and practice it consistently, we will open the door to miraculous encounters on a regular basis. If we want to do the "greater works" Jesus spoke of, we must first embrace the greatest work: prayer!

Prayer Warriors, Arise!

It is time for all prophetic intercessors and prayer warriors to arise. It is time for us to stand up and take our place in the kingdom of God. I believe that the earth is groaning in anticipation of the manifestation of the sons of God. (See Romans 8:19.) A warrior is a brave, experienced soldier or fighter; a *prayer* warrior is someone who boldly takes up the mantle of intercession and stands in the gap for his or her generation. I don't know about you, but I am tired of hearing complaints about the negative things going on in the world. It is futile to complain when we have the supernatural at our disposal. Jesus may be coming back soon, but that doesn't mean we should leave society in a worse state than it was in when He went away.

At one point in our lives, my wife and I resided in a neighborhood that was overrun with crime. The home across the street from us was a crack house as well as the headquarters of a prostitution ring. In fact, our neighborhood was known to have one of the highest concentrations of prostitutes in our city. Not wanting to exacerbate the situation, I didn't bother praying about it at first—until the Lord opened my eyes. He showed me that we didn't have to accept or tolerate what was going on around us—we could change it! My wife and I took our places in prayer and began to call those things that are not as though they were, according to Romans 4:17. To our utter amazement, the crack house across the street shut down in a matter of weeks. Glory to God!

How many crack houses need to close down in your city? How many prostitution rings need to be dismantled in your state? You have the power and authority to bring change to those situations. You don't need a seminary degree or a ministerial license to be a prayer warrior. Jesus gave you permission to pray when He said, *"And whatsoever ye shall ask in my name, that will I do, that the Father may be glorified in the Son"* (John 14:13). You can't complain that nothing is happening in your life if you haven't been praying!

It is not enough to simply pray. We must also have faith that what we have prayed will come to pass. I personally believe that prayer is one of the most underrated activities of the New Testament. The patriarchs of the faith longed for a day when they could enjoy the kind of communion with God that you and I are entitled to have. Let us not disappoint the great cloud of witnesses who have gone before us. Their mantle is upon us now, and it behooves us to make a difference in this world. Remember, prayer is prophetic; therefore, every time we pray, we are prophesying. What do we want to see manifested in our lives? Which doors do we believe God will open in our lives? *Now* is the time to release our faith and to pray without ceasing.

We talk a lot about the works of Jesus, but the thing Jesus spent most of His time doing was praying. Why? Because there is nothing more powerful and valuable than communion with the Father. Everything that we do, as believers, is birthed out of that relationship. Everything Jesus did, every miracle He performed, was birthed out of His intimacy with God. Jesus said, *"I am the vine, ye are the branches: he that abideth in me, and I in him, the same bringeth forth much fruit: for without me ye can do nothing"* (John 15:5). We must abide in the vine through prayer. This is the key to fruitfulness.

He Has Prepared a Place for Us!

The gospel of John records what Jesus taught His disciples about the Father. This is very important, because, at this point in the gospel account, He was about to be crucified. He said to His disciples,

> *Let not your heart be troubled: ye believe in God, believe also in me. In my Father's house are many mansions: if it were not so, I would have told you. I go to prepare a place for you. And if I go and prepare a place for you, I will come again, and receive you unto myself; that where I am, there ye may be also.* (John 14:1–3)

Growing up in the church, I heard this passage of Scripture quoted many times, always in reference to heaven. While I believe that Jesus was making reference to the life to come, I also believe His words are relevant for the here and now. Jesus knew that His death would likely cause the disciples to fear and worry, and He wanted them to be prepared, spiritually.

Jesus used an interesting word in this passage: *"mansions."* He was not talking about preparing for us Beverly Hills mansions with palm trees; He was referring to "rooms" or "dwelling places." As a metaphor for intimacy and fellowship with God, the term carries a dual meaning. On the one hand, it means that Jesus went into the heavenly realm to prepare for us dwelling places in heaven. On the other hand, it means that He has prepared for us a place of intimacy with the Father—right here, right now. Through Jesus, we have a permanent dwelling place in God's house. The sacrifice of Jesus on the cross, and our receipt of that sacrifice by faith, has secured for us an eternal position of fellowship and intimacy with God. He desires to commune with us on a regular basis. This is one of the greatest miracles of the New Testament! We who were afar off from God can now come near to Him through the blood of Christ.

WE DON'T HAVE TO WAIT UNTIL WE GET TO HEAVEN TO HAVE INTIMACY WITH GOD; WE CAN HAVE INTIMACY WITH HIM RIGHT NOW.

For centuries, much of the church has believed that the Christian's life on this earth is simply obscure and irrelevant as he or she suffers for Christ's sake, waiting for eternity. But this is not the pattern that Jesus left for His church. Eternal life is not just what happens when you die; rather, you received eternal life at the moment of salvation. The Bible says, *"And this is **life eternal**, that **they might know thee the only true God, and Jesus Christ**, whom thou hast sent"* (John 17:3). The word for *"know"* here is the Greek word *ginōskō*, which is an idiomatic expression for intimacy. This means that true eternal life is characterized by deep intimacy with God. The most unfortunate thing that can happen to a believer is getting to heaven and meeting the Lord for the first time. When we get to heaven, we should not be meeting Him for the first time; we should be reuniting with the Lover of our souls! We should be familiar with His voice and acclimated to His touch. If prayer on earth is an inconvenience to us, then we might have a serious problem when we get to heaven. I don't know about you, but I don't want to wait to die before I really live; I want to know the Lord right now!

Prayer Brings Supernatural Release

There is no question that the first-century church was familiar with the power and presence of God. I find it fascinating how God used a bunch of fishermen and misfits to turn the world upside down. This encourages me, because it reminds me that the Lord can use anyone to fulfill His purposes. The apostle Peter underwent a complete transformation upon receiving the baptism of the Holy Spirit—no longer a coward, he was a man full of the power of God. As the church experienced increasing signs, wonders, and miracles, the persecution of the devil intensified. This escalation was very visible in the days of the apostles:

> *Now about that time Herod the king stretched forth his hands to vex certain of the church. And he killed James the brother of John with the sword. And because he saw it pleased the Jews, he proceeded further to take Peter also. (Then were the days of unleavened bread.) And when he had apprehended him, he put him in prison, and delivered him to four quaternions of soldiers to keep him; intending after Easter to bring*

him forth to the people. Peter therefore was kept in prison: but prayer was made without ceasing of the church unto God for him.

(Acts 12:1–5)

As a form of retaliation against the miracles, signs, and wonders they were walking in, Herod began to attack, imprison, and even kill key leaders in the church. He even captured Peter with the intention of executing him. But God had other plans. The Bible says that prayer was made without ceasing on Peter's behalf. This fact gives us a glimpse of the importance of prayer in the early church.

PRAYER HAS THE POWER TO BRING SUPERNATURAL RELEASE TO ANY AREA OF OUR LIVES.

At a time when most people would have been fretting or seeking physical vindication, the church was fully engaged in prayer and intercession. In face of the enemy's attacks, the believers were not distracted but instead intensified their prayer lives. Why? Because they understood the supernatural power of prayer. As they continued to pray for Peter, something began to shift in the spiritual realm:

And when Herod would have brought him forth, the same night Peter was sleeping between two soldiers, bound with two chains: and the keepers before the door kept the prison. And, behold, the angel of the Lord came upon him, and a light shined in the prison: and he smote Peter on the side, and raised him up, saying, Arise up quickly. And his chains fell off from his hands. And the angel said unto him, Gird thyself, and bind on thy sandals. And so he did. And he saith unto him, Cast thy garment about thee, and follow me. (Acts 12:6–8)

This passage is a testimony to the power of prayer to break any form of bondage in your life. What miracle are you expecting? Prayer will release God's miraculous power in your life.

Bondage-Breaking Prayer

Heavenly Father, I come to You in the name of Your Son, Jesus. I acknowledge Jesus as my Lord and Savior, and I ask You to forgive me and to cleanse me from all sin, both known and unknown. I renounce all powers of sin, darkness, bondage, and addiction that are operating in my life, and I declare that He whom the Son makes free is free indeed, according to John 8:36. Today, I receive freedom in my life. I declare that all negative life-controlling issues are broken, in the name of Jesus. I receive Your supernatural strength to walk in victory in every area of my life: spirit, soul, and body. Every curse is broken, and every heavy burden is lifted by reason of the anointing in Jesus' name. Amen!

Prophetic Prayer

Father, I thank You that Your Word declares I will do the works of Jesus, and even greater works. I thank You for giving me access to You through prayer in Jesus' name. I declare that every barrier or stronghold in my life is torn down by the power of the Holy Spirit and that I live a miraculous life in You. I am a magnet for miracles—they are commonplace to me! I thank You that I don't have to wait until I get to heaven to have intimacy with You; I can walk in unbroken fellowship and intimacy with the Father here and now. I declare that I experience supernatural release in every area of my life. I am completely reliant upon You, Father, for Your strength and power in my life. In Jesus' name, amen!

Prophetic Insights

1. What did Jesus mean when He said that God would "make His abode" with believers? (See John 14.)

2. How did the early believers in the book of Acts respond to persecution, and what does their response teach us today?

3. Is there any form of evil or bondage in your life that you have accepted and tolerated? If so, take it before the Lord in prayer, and then watch as He sets you free.

12

Accessing the Heavenly Realm

And [God] hath raised us up together, and made us sit together in
heavenly places *in Christ Jesus.*
—Ephesians 2:6

Whether you realize it or not, we, as born-again believers, are seated with Christ in heavenly places. You may be saying to yourself, *How can this be?* I'm glad you asked! The moment we accepted Jesus into our hearts, our lives became hidden in Him. This is what the apostle Paul was referring to in his epistle to the Colossians, where he wrote:

> *If ye then be risen with Christ, seek those things which are above, where Christ sitteth on the right hand of God. Set your affection on things above, not on things on the earth. For ye are dead, and **your life is hid with Christ in God**. When Christ, who is our life, shall appear, then shall ye also appear with him in glory.* (Colossians 3:1–4)

In the same way that a person hides his or her valuables in a safe, our lives are concealed in Jesus. The more passionately we seek Him, the better our understanding will be of who we are. Most believers are ignorant of the truth that they are seated with Christ in the heavenly realm. How can we be seated with Christ while we are still very present on the earth? Because, although we are physically here on earth, we are spiritually seated with Christ—meaning we have unlimited access to the heavenly realm. It also means we possess the same authority as Jesus. When it comes to prophetic prayer, it is important that we pray from the right position. Again, many believers pray from a position of defeat rather than of victory. Beloved, this is not the will of God for our lives.

PRAYER IS AN OPPORTUNITY TO DISCOVER YOUR DIVINE IDENTITY. GOD IS WAITING TO REVEAL WHO YOU ARE!

Many years ago, software engineers developed a method of virtual data storage now known as "cloud technology." We no longer need to hunt around the house for a physical device to store our information—we can simply back up the data in the cloud! Through this technology, we are able to access our files twenty-four hours a day, seven days a week.

Our spiritual lives are not all that different. Through prayer, we have unlimited access to the heavenly realm. We can receive wisdom, knowledge, healing, and revelation directly from heaven. In fact, prayer is our divine passport into the heavenly realm. This is an amazing reality of the born-again life. Most believers are accustomed to prayers of petition, by which we ask God to meet a particular need; but many believers are not accustomed to praying from a heavenly position. Remember, we are seated with Christ in heavenly places! This means we can actually pray from heaven rather than just look up at the sky, as if wishing and hoping our request will be granted. We can pray in a posture of confidence, faith, and intimacy with God. Every time we come before God, we know that we belong because we have accepted our position in heavenly places.

Intimacy with the Holy Spirit

The famous healing evangelist Kathryn Kuhlman (1907–1976) was a champion of the Holy Spirit and a great general of the faith. In her healing meetings, she would often say, "Don't grieve the Holy Spirit! Don't you know He's all I got?" I love this statement, and I love that she was unafraid to display her reliance on the Holy Spirit. It probably seemed strange to many of the attendees, but there was no denying her love for the Holy Spirit. I am very adamant about the need for studying the Word of God, as you have probably realized by now, but I believe there is also a great need in the body of Christ for a new revelation of the Holy Spirit. Our effectiveness as prophetic intercessors hinges on intimacy with the Holy Spirit.

In my book *Kingdom Authority*, I describe the orphan spirit, which is a spirit of fear and insecurity that comes from not knowing one's identity in Christ. I have found that almost every form of bondage in the believer's life is connected in some way to the orphan spirit. Before we can embrace prayer and reap its benefits, we must learn who we are in Christ. The only way to know who we are in Christ is to develop an intimate relationship with the Holy Spirit. In fact, intimacy with the Holy Spirit is the key to living a supernatural life. Jesus told us, *"Howbeit when he, the Spirit of **truth**, is come, he will guide you into **all truth**: for he shall not speak of himself; but whatsoever he shall hear, that shall he speak: and he will shew you things to come"* (John 16:13). The Holy Spirit reveals the truth of who we are in Christ. And this revelation gives us confidence in our relationship with God.

Heavenly Wisdom and Revelation

More than ever before, the body of Christ needs supernatural wisdom to navigate the perilous times in which we live. As Paul prayed in the book of Ephesians,

> That the God of our Lord Jesus Christ, the Father of glory, may give
> unto you the spirit of wisdom and revelation in the knowledge of him:
> the **eyes of your understanding** being enlightened; that ye may know

what is the hope of his calling, and what the riches of the glory of his
inheritance in the saints.   (Ephesians 1:17–18)

God wants to give us heavenly wisdom. By heavenly wisdom, we are referring to the application of divine knowledge to matters in the earth. Heavenly wisdom is full, complete, and divine. We need it in order to relate to our spouses, to raise our children, and to operate in the marketplace. This wisdom is available to us; we simply need to activate it by faith. Every time we approach the throne of grace through prayer, we are accessing the wisdom of God.

Along with wisdom, we also need revelation. What is revelation? The word "revelation" comes from the Greek word *apokalypsis*, which means "laying bare, making naked, a disclosure of truth." Simply put, revelation is the unveiling of something that was previously unknown. God wants to reveal things to us, His children, that will benefit us in both the natural and spiritual realms.

I will never forget the first time God gave me a revelation through prayer about something in His Word. It was as if God pulled back a curtain in my mind, allowing me to see clearly. Once you have received revelation, you find it impossible to continue on the same path you were traveling before that truth was revealed.

The Revealer of Secrets

Paul's prayer in Ephesians 1:17–18 is one of my favorite prayers of the Bible, and I believe that it is just as relevant today as it was for the church at Ephesus. It is God's earnest desire that you and I receive the spirit of wisdom and revelation in the knowledge of Him. In other words, He wants to be known by us! In an earlier chapter, we established that to know God is to have eternal life. Yet the only way we can know an omnipotent, omniscient God is by revelation. I believe that there are things He wants to divulge to us on a regular basis. This is why prayer should be an important part of our daily lives. Imagine you are taking an open-book test, and all the correct answers are printed in your book in chronological order. Will you pass the test? Of course! The only way to fail that kind of a test would be by neglecting to open your book. Sadly, many believers are failing the tests of life because they refuse to open the Book with all the answers—the Word of God—and to devote themselves to prayer.

When I was a kid, I had a friend who seemed to somehow know everything about everyone at all times. If you wanted to find out the latest information, all you had to do was give this kid a call. Well, God is like that friend of mine—He knows literally everything about everyone in the universe, because He created everyone in the universe! If you want to know something, simply ask Him. He promises to show us what we need to know: *"The secret of the LORD is with them that fear him; and he will shew them his covenant"* (Psalm 25:14). God wants to reveal to you and me the secrets of His heart. He wants to show us things about Himself that we have yet to discover. He also wants to expose the plans of the enemy for our lives so that we might walk in constant victory.

PRAYER IS MORE THAN A ONE-WAY CONVERSATION; IT IS A DIVINE CONSULTATION WHEREBY GOD DIVULGES SUPERNATURAL INFORMATION TO THE BELIEVER.

Once we receive wisdom and revelation from God, the second part of Paul's prayer in the book of Ephesians will be realized: *"The eyes of your understanding being enlightened; that ye may know what is the hope of his calling, and what the riches of the glory of his inheritance in the saints"* (Ephesians 1:18). The word for *"enlightened"* here is a very powerful term that comes from the Greek *phōtizō*, "to give light, to shine,…to bring to light, render evident." From it, we derive the English word "photograph"—a picture that is captured by a camera, in which an image is focused onto film or other light-sensitive material and then made visible and permanent by chemical treatment. Every time we pray earnestly, with the intent to receive revelation from God, a picture is burned on our hearts—a picture we can neither forget nor deny. Even when the present circumstances seem to contradict what we have heard from God in prayer, the picture is still there, resonating in our hearts. God wants to bring illumination to every area of darkness, fear, and discouragement in our lives. Illumination produces hope, because once we have a picture of God's plan for our lives, we become hopeful of the future. You could say that illumination produces expectation, and expectation is the breeding ground for manifestation. Prayerful people are in a constant state of expectancy because they are anticipating seeing miracles happen in their lives. There are riches and treasures within us that God wants to reveal. Hallelujah!

The Three Manifestations of the Supernatural

Earlier, I identified three dimensions of prayer: the outer court, the inner court, and the Holy of Holies. Since prayer opens us to the supernatural, it is important to understand the various realms of the supernatural. I believe that there are three primary manifestations (or dimensions) of the supernatural that the praying believer will encounter: (1) faith, (2) the anointing, and (3) the glory of God.

1. Faith

The first manifestation of the supernatural is faith. Just as the Israelites had to enter the gate of the tabernacle through the outer court, you and I must approach God through the gate of faith in order to enter the supernatural. The Bible says, *"Now faith is the substance of things hoped for, the evidence of things not seen"* (Hebrews 11:1). Faith is the substance, the foundation, of the supernatural. It is the foundation of the prophetic. Every encounter with God in a believer's life is based on faith in the Word of God.

Many people desire to have encounters with God, but they are frustrated and discouraged, because they lack a biblical understanding of faith. Every house must be built on a solid foundation, or it will collapse. Many believers are experiencing a spiritual collapse because they lack the solid foundation of the Word of God. Faith is a revelation of the truth and integrity of God's Word that brings conviction to the heart of the believer. For example, if you have faith in the Word of God in the area of healing, it means you have a revelation of God's power and desire to heal any and all sickness. When you pray for the sick, you are confident they will get well, because you are convinced that Christ is the Healer. When you pray for those with a financial need, you are confident all their needs will be met, because you are convinced that Christ is the Provider. Faith is unmistakable and undeniable! You can't pretend to have it or conjure it up in your mind; it is not mere mental assent. Faith is conviction.

There are many blessings, promises, and other manifestations of God's power that are based solely upon the faith of the believer. I remember praying over my daughter once when she was extremely sick. I didn't feel any goose bumps or tingles on the back of my neck; I simply claimed 1 Peter 2:24 on my daughter's behalf. Shortly thereafter, my daughter received her healing. Glory to God! If you truly want to experience the benefits of prophetic prayer in your life, you first must learn to release your faith in God's Word. The more of the Word of God you have inside you, the stronger your faith will become; the stronger your faith, the more effective your prayers; and the more effective your prayers, the more supernatural results you will see. The Bible says, *"But without faith it is impossible to please [God]: for he that cometh to God must believe that he is, and that he is a rewarder of them that diligently seek him"* (Hebrews 11:6).

2. The Anointing

The second manifestation of the supernatural is the anointing, which corresponds to the inner court of the Old Testament. The word "anointing," in its primary New Testament usage, comes from the Greek word *chrisma*, which means "anything smeared on, unguent, ointment." As we mentioned earlier, in the Old Testament, the anointing referred to the aromatic oil used to inaugurate the priests; in the New Testament, the anointing represents the presence and power of the Holy Spirit operating in and upon the believer:

> *But the anointing which ye have received of him abideth in you, and ye need not that any man teach you: but as the same anointing teacheth you of all things, and is truth, and is no lie, and even as it hath taught you, ye shall abide in him.*   (1 John 2:27)

The anointing teaches, equips, empowers, and enables believers to do what they have been called to do.

I like to define the anointing as the yoke-destroying, burden-removing power of God in your life. Jesus was well acquainted with the anointing. As He said,

> *The Spirit of the Lord is upon me, because he hath anointed me to preach the gospel to the poor; he hath sent me to heal the brokenhearted, to preach deliverance to the captives, and recovering of sight to the blind, to set at liberty them that are bruised, to preach the acceptable year of the Lord.* (Luke 4:18–19)

It was through the anointing that Jesus healed the sick, raised the dead, cast out demons, and proclaimed the gospel of the kingdom of God.

Later, Peter would preach about *"how God anointed Jesus of Nazareth with the Holy Spirit and with power: who went about doing good, and healing all that were oppressed of the devil; for God was with him"* (Acts 10:38). In other words, to be able to flow in the power of God, Jesus had to believe that He was anointed. Faith allows us to believe the same. Every time we pray in the Holy Spirit, we are tapping into the supernatural anointing of God. We need the anointing to be God's witnesses. We need the anointing to share the gospel. And we need the anointing to survive in this world. If we are born again, we have the Holy Spirit living within us, which means we already possess the anointing.

When I first became a believer, I remember hearing Christian television ministers talk about the anointing. They always said that there was a price to pay for the anointing, and I thought to myself, *How much does it cost?* I didn't realize that the blood of Jesus gave me the right to receive the anointing of the Holy Spirit. Beloved, you are already anointed! You simply need to release your anointing by acting on the Word of God in faith.

THE ANOINTING IS THE YOKE-DESTROYING, BURDEN-REMOVING POWER OF GOD IN A BELIEVER'S LIFE.

Without the anointing, we are simply operating in our own strength and by our own faith. It takes supernatural faith and anointing to bring about deliverance in our lives. Faith is the revelation, and the anointing is the power to manifest that which has been revealed. Without faith, there is no revelation; and without the anointing, there is no power. But when you combine faith with the anointing, you have a supernatural powder keg ready to explode. The anointing is both tangible—you can feel it—and transferable, able to move from person to person.

3. The Glory of God

In the Old Testament, the greatest manifestation of the presence of God was experienced within the Holy of Holies. This is where the *shekinah* glory was revealed. Under the law, no one was qualified to stand in the manifest presence of God; Moses was the only exception. (See Exodus 34:29–35.) The glory of God is the highest dimension of the supernatural because it is the manifest presence of God. Every time the glory of God is revealed, something supernatural happens. When His glory is manifested, miracles, signs, and wonders happen instantly. Time is at once suspended and accelerated.

I have had many personal encounters with the glory of God. One night, while I was worshipping God, the glory of God invaded my room. I could not speak or move for minutes (it felt like hours). All I could do was weep with my mouth wide open. One thing is certain: I was forever changed by this encounter.

Moses prayed, *"I beseech thee, shew me thy glory"* (Exodus 33:18), but the Lord told Moses that no man could see Him and live. (See verse 20.) The glory of God is both tangible and visible. Many times, when people experience the glory of God, they feel a sense of heaviness. This is because the presence of God has "weight" to it! The Bible says that Jesus was raised from the dead by the glory of the Father. (See Romans 6:4.) I believe that the glory of God invaded the underworld and raised Christ from the dead. The glory of God has the ability to raise dead things to life again. When we are in the glory dimension, faith and the anointing become obsolete. I can almost imagine what heaven will be like, based on my encounters with the glory of God. When the glory of God manifests, there is unlimited revelation.

Prophetic Prayer

Father, I thank You that through Your Son, Jesus, I have been given unlimited access to the heavenly realm. I recognize that prayer is a divine privilege extended to me under the new covenant. Thank You for creating in me a hunger for Your presence. I delight in experiencing You. Through faith and prayer, I will access all three dimensions of the supernatural. I declare that my spirit man is open and receptive to the revelation of the Holy Spirit. I know that I am seated with You in heavenly places; therefore, I proclaim that I have victory in every area of my life. I live in the faith, peace, and prosperity of God every day. I walk in the supernatural on a daily basis, and I provoke others around me to do the same. I thank You that the anointing of the Holy Spirit destroys every yoke (bondage) operating in my life. I walk under an open heaven and the manifestation of Your glory in my life, in Jesus' name! Amen.

Prophetic Insights

1. How can we have heavenly wisdom?

2. What are the three manifestations of the supernatural that the praying believer will encounter?

3. Which of these manifestations do you notice the most in your life? The least?

PROPHETIC PRACTICUM

1. Use your imagination: How could your life could be better? Where could God do a mighty work? What miracles do you want to see manifested in your life? Which doors do you believe God will open to you? Release the power for these events by praying prophetically for them.

2. Pray the bondage-breaking prayer over any specific sins, bondages, and addictions in your life.

3. Find a fellow Christian who is seeking to pray in the Spirit, and take turns sharing your stories and experiences relating to the three primary manifestations of the supernatural: faith, the anointing, and the glory of God. Then, rejoice together!

13

Teach Us to Pray

And it came to pass, that, as [Jesus] was praying in a certain place,
*when he ceased, one of his disciples said unto him, Lord, **teach us to***
***pray**, as John also taught his disciples.*
—Luke 11:1

Prayer is obviously a critical component to walking in the supernatural and releasing one's destiny. The question remains: how can we learn to pray effectively, i.e., according to the will of God? We discussed earlier how prayer follows a pattern based on the Old Testament tabernacle. But what is the pattern of prayer in the New Testament? In the gospel of Luke, the disciples made a profound request of Jesus: *"Lord, teach us to pray"* (Luke 11:1). Why did the disciples consider prayer of such importance? Because prayer was paramount to Jesus' earthly ministry. The disciples witnessed this phenomenon every day they walked with Him. They knew that if they were ever truly going to follow in His footsteps, they would need to emulate His prayer life. And so He told them,

When ye pray, say, Our Father which art in heaven, hallowed be thy
name. Thy kingdom come. Thy will be done, as in heaven, so in earth.

> *Give us day by day our daily bread. And forgive us our sins; for we also forgive every one that is indebted to us. And lead us not into temptation; but deliver us from evil.* (Luke 11:2–4)

The gospel of Matthew records the same prayer with slightly different wording:

> *Our Father which art in heaven, hallowed be thy name. Thy kingdom come. Thy will be done in earth, as it is in heaven. Give us this day our daily bread. And forgive us our debts, as we forgive our debtors. And lead us not into temptation, but deliver us from evil: for thine is the kingdom, and the power, and the glory, for ever. Amen.* (Matthew 6:9–13)

The Kingdom Protocol of Prayer

The above two passages are often referred to as "The Lord's Prayer." But the prayer Jesus prayed wasn't actually for the Lord; it was a prayer for the disciples! When we learn to follow the kingdom pattern of prayer, as revealed by our Lord, we will see our prayers produce more and more results. Remember, prayer is, by nature, prophetic, just as we believers are, by nature, prophetic. The more we embrace the prophetic nature of prayer, the more manifestations of prayer we will see. Prayer, like everything else in the kingdom of God, follows a protocol—it operates according to a specific set of rules, or guidelines. Jesus instructed His disciples to pray according to the following pattern:

Acknowledge God as our Father.

First of all, we are told to acknowledge and embrace the *Fatherhood* of God. When we see God as our Father rather than just some impersonal deity in the clouds, we are enabled to connect with Him in a very deep, intimate way. The apostle Paul made it very clear that we are, after all, His children:

> *For as many as are led by the Spirit of God, they are the sons of God. For ye have not received the spirit of bondage again to fear; but ye*

have received the Spirit of adoption, whereby we cry, Abba, Father. The Spirit itself beareth witness with our spirit, that we are the children of God. (Romans 8:14–16)

Whether you know it or not, you are a child of God, and He loves you unconditionally.

Recognize that God is in heaven.

The second step in the model prayer is to acknowledge that God is exalted in the heavens. This is a form of worship, but it doesn't mean that we have to see Him as afar off; remember, we are seated with Christ in heavenly places (see Ephesians 2:6), and we have already been blessed in Him. By acknowledging that God is in heaven, we recognize that He is not limited by the constraints and confines of this world's system. We are also acknowledging that we are not of this world, either!

Glorify God's name as holy.

Regardless of our eschatological or theological view, one thing that we should consider irrefutable is the truth that God is a holy God. He is holy! His *name* is holy! This is important to keep in mind when we pray, because we have been graced to be able to call upon His name. This is no light matter. In the Old Testament, the name of God was ineffable; but in the New Testament, through the name of Jesus, we can call upon the Father without shame, guilt, condemnation, or fear. Hallelujah!

Declare that God's kingdom must be manifest.

Most people in the Western world have no concept of a king or a kingdom, but it is important to remember that God is the King of the universe, and He also happens to be our heavenly Father. Every earthly king is interested in the advancement of his kingdom. In the same way, it is God's highest priority to manifest His kingdom in the earthly realm. Every time we pray, we must deliberately pray for His kingdom to be manifested and advanced in the earth.

Declare that God's will must be done...

What is the will of God? The Greek word for "will" can be translated as "what one wishes or has determined shall be done." When we pray, we ought to be concerned about God's will for our lives and the lives of the people around us—what He desires and determines to see done. Have you ever prayed and asked God to show you His will for a particular area of your life? It has been said that the safest place to be is in the will of God. When we are deeply concerned with the will of God, we enjoy greater levels of joy and contentment.

On earth as it is in heaven.

Earlier, we talked about the responsibility of every believer to colonize the earth through prayer. Our prayer closet is literally a supernatural embassy of the kingdom of God on the earth. God desires to "heaven-form" the earth so that it begins to resemble heaven. The next time you pray, declare that the culture, atmosphere, and attitude of heaven must invade your life. There is a need for heaven to invade the earth in these desperate times. What would happen if our homes, churches, schools, communities, and cities begin to look and function like heaven? I believe that people would flock into the house of God like never before. When cultivating the earth with the atmosphere of heaven becomes a priority of our prayer lives, we will experience answered prayer on a consistent basis.

Ask for your daily bread.

The Scripture is very clear: "*Ask, and it shall be given you; seek, and ye shall find; knock, and it shall be opened unto you*" (Matthew 7:7). There is definitely a place in prayer for petitions. In fact, God wants us to ask Him for things. Contrary to popular belief, praying for material things is encouraged in Scripture. In the Greek, the tense of the above verse is imperative, meaning that Jesus essentially told His disciples to demand their daily bread from God. As God's children, we have a covenant with Him. And the Bible tells us that healing and provision are His children's bread. (See, for example, Mark 7:27.)

Ask for forgiveness of known sins.

I have heard it said that Christians no longer have to ask for forgiveness because the blood of Jesus covers their sins. This is a gross misunderstanding of Scripture. Despite what some modern-day Christians claim, New Testament believers are encouraged to acknowledge their sins and failures before God. Though it is true that the blood of Jesus covers our sins, we are still responsible to acknowledge wrongdoing when the Holy Spirit brings it to our attention. In fact, the Bible says, *"If we **confess our sins**, he is faithful and just to forgive us our sins, and to cleanse us from all unrighteousness"* (1 John 1:9). Repentance of sin keeps our hearts pure before God and enables us to hear His voice clearly.

Release those who have wronged you.

It is very important that you and I learn to release those who have wounded or otherwise hurt us. This process includes releasing people from their debts. The Bible commands us, *"And be ye kind one to another, tenderhearted, forgiving one another, even as God for Christ's sake hath forgiven you"* (Ephesians 4:32). The more we learn to release others through forgiveness in prayer, the more we will walk in freedom. Remember, an unforgiving person is a bitter person, and a bitter person is a barren person.

Pray to avoid temptation.

The truth is that temptation is a very real part of the Christian life. Most times, we are not aware of all the temptations in our path on any given day. But the good news is that there is no temptation we face that is uncommon to man, and God will always provide a way out, if we will only trust His power:

> *There hath no temptation taken you but such as is common to man: but God is faithful, who will not suffer you to be tempted above that ye are able; but will with the temptation also make a way to escape, that ye may be able to bear it.* (1 Corinthians 10:13)

Some people think that this is an "old-fashioned" idea, but it is wise to pray that the Lord would deliver us from evil and danger, seen and unseen.

I cannot tell you how many times God has warned me about something before it happened, either in order to prepare me or to enable me to avoid it altogether. Oh, what a gracious God we serve!

Attribute to God the kingdom, the power, and the glory.

I've said before that prayer has the power to change the atmosphere around us. That is because prayer is an extension of God's kingdom in the earth. The kingdom is threefold in its manifestation in the earth; therefore, we must acknowledge this threefold reality when we pray.

1. The Kingdom

The kingdom of God is the government of God. The word "kingdom" comes from the Greek word *basileia*, which means "kingship, dominion, rule." God's kingdom is His sovereignty made manifest in every sphere of society. By acknowledging God's kingdom, we are recognizing His rule and dominion in every area of our lives. This is a matter of submitting, or coming under His authority. Many believers do not have a revelation of God's kingship, and this is the very reason their prayers are impotent and powerless. As we submit to His authority, the authority we walk in expands.

2. The Power

The power of God, as outlined in the Lord's model prayer, is the ability of God to do the supernatural. God's kingdom is a domain of power made manifest. When we pray *"For thine is the power,"* we release the supernatural ability of God into whatever situation we are facing. The meaning behind the Greek word for "power," *dunamis*, is profound: "inherent power, power residing in a thing by virtue of its nature...power for performing miracles." I challenge you to pray this prayer: "Lord, I release Your kingdom power in every area of my life right now, in Jesus' name. I declare that Your strength and miraculous power invade every circumstance that lies before me, in Jesus' name. Amen!"

3. The Glory

When Jesus mentioned the glory of God in His model prayer, He was referring to the atmosphere and culture of heaven—the tangible manifestation of heaven's environment on the earth. Earlier, we noted that the glory of God was the highest dimension of the supernatural. Once the glory of God is revealed, divine activity is ignited. The more we cultivate the atmosphere of heaven through prayer, the more supernatural manifestations we will see.

At our church, we started a Saturday evening service of prayer, worship, and intercession. It is amazing how many people have testified that they feel the tangible presence of God the moment they step into the sanctuary. Why is this experience so common? Because our congregation has learned to cultivate an atmosphere that is conducive to the presence and glory of God. Every time we gather to worship or to hear from God's Word, something supernatural happens. The same can be true of your church, your home, or any other place. It starts by recognizing God's presence. Once you recognize His presence, you can reverence Him. And with recognition and reverence, there is release. You and I can live under an open heaven all the days of our lives.

Prophetic Prayer

Father, in the name of Jesus, I thank You for teaching me the kingdom pattern of prayer and intercession. Thank You for being a loving and gracious Father who knows everything about me, yet still loves me. I pray now that Your kingdom would come, and Your will would be done, in the earth as it is in heaven. I declare that my atmosphere is impregnated with the glory of God. I have literally become infected by Your presence, and I will take this wonderful presence with me wherever I go. Thank You, Lord, for the manifestation of Your supernatural power in my life. I release Your power now, by faith in Your Word, and I thank You in advance for signs, wonders, and miracles. Let Your *shekinah* glory fall upon me now, in the mighty name of Jesus. Amen!

Prophetic Insights

1. Where can we find our pattern for prayer?

2. What is the threefold manifestation of the kingdom on earth, and how does that impact believers?

3. How can you incorporate this threefold pattern into your prayers?

14

The Power of Effectual Prayer

Confess your faults one to another, and pray one for another, that ye may be healed. The effectual fervent prayer of a righteous man availeth much.
—James 5:16

To me, one of the most profound stories in the Old Testament is the story of the prophet Elijah recorded in the book of 1 Kings 17. It begins like this:

> And Elijah the Tishbite, who was of the inhabitants of Gilead, said unto Ahab, As the LORD God of Israel liveth, before whom I stand, there shall not be dew nor rain these years, but according to my word.
>
> (1 Kings 17:1)

Can you believe this? I hope you do, because it's in the Bible! One man in Israel stopped the rain for three and a half years. The significance of his act was recognized all the way through to the New Testament, where the apostle James wrote:

> Confess your faults one to another, and pray one for another, that ye may be healed. The effectual fervent prayer of a righteous man availeth

much. Elias [another name for Elijah] *was a man subject to like passions as we are, and he prayed earnestly that it might not rain: and it rained not on the earth by the space of three years and six months. And he prayed again, and the heaven gave rain, and the earth brought forth her fruit.* (James 5:16–18)

We have stated numerous times throughout this book that prayer is powerful. But that is a serious understatement. Not only is prayer powerful; it is absolutely necessary. Every time we pray, something happens. The apostle James said that the *"effectual fervent prayer"* of the righteous avails much. (See James 5:16.) The *Amplified Version* states it this way:

Confess to one another therefore your faults (your slips, your false steps, your offenses, your sins) and pray [also] for one another, that you may be healed and restored [to a spiritual tone of mind and heart]. The earnest (heartfelt, continued) prayer of a righteous man makes tremendous power available [dynamic in its working]. (James 5:16 AMP)

There is tremendous power available in prayer! There is enough power in prayer to close up the heavens over an entire nation. What would happen if you and I began to embrace the power of prayer wholeheartedly? I believe that our communities would be forever transformed by the glory of God. If one man could stop the rain in ancient Palestine, can you imagine the impact of an entire church praying over our nation?

PROPHETIC PRAYER IS BOTH THE RIGHT AND THE RESPONSIBILITY OF EVERY BORN-AGAIN BELIEVER.

In the Old Testament, the prophet was seen as an oracle of God who carried a special anointing to prophesy and perform miracles. But the Scriptures say that we can see the same results as the prophet Elijah did in our own lives. We don't need a special designation or calling in order to affect the heavens with our prayers. All we need to do is recognize the supernatural power of prayer and begin to declare the Word of God from our prayer closets.

Pray with All Your Heart

Again, the Bible says, *"The **effectual** fervent prayer of a righteous man availeth much"* (James 5:16). What does *"effectual"* mean? In Greek, it's *energeō*, which means "to be operative, be at work, put forth power." This is where we get our English word *energy*. Every time we pray prophetically, there is a release of supernatural power and energy. The key to seeing the manifestation of our prayers is to pray with all our heart, for this releases the supernatural power of God. Think of the way an airplane takes off. In order for the plane to ascend into the air, it must draw enough power from the jet engines. In the same manner, if we want to see our prayers "take off," we have to pray with earnest, heartfelt desire. This is the spiritual fuel that powers our prayer lives.

Many people pray, but they don't pray with all their hearts. To pray with all one's heart is to pray without a contingency plan or an alternative in mind. It is to pray with an attitude of expectancy. Have you ever prayed for someone, yet, in the back of your mind, you weren't completely convinced that something would happen? People pray like this all the time! Religion has taught us to see prayer as some sort of spiritual exercise or moral duty, but this is not what the Scriptures teach us. The people whose prayers are recorded in the Bible prayed as if their lives depended it. They weren't just trying to fulfill some moral or ethical responsibility; they were literally crying out in desperation to see the power of God manifested in their lives. If we want to see results, we have to pray the same way. It is the energetic, heartfelt prayer that yields results.

WHEN WE PRAY,
GOD DOESN'T SIMPLY LISTEN TO OUR WORDS;
HE LOOKS AT THE CONDITION OF OUR HEARTS.

How many blessings and breakthroughs have we missed out on because we failed to pray with all our heart? Imagine a couple is going out on a blind date, and the first thing the guy says to the girl is, "If this date doesn't work out, I have someone else I can call." I think it would be safe to assume that the date probably won't go too well! Why? Because the man is not fully committed to the woman in front of him. He's not prepared to give her all his time, energy, and affection.

Many people do the same thing to God in prayer. They pray, but they have a "backup plan" just in case their prayer doesn't yield the desired results. They pray for the healing of an illness, but they have their doctor's phone number and their medicine cabinets as backup just in case God doesn't answer them. If we make a habit of coming to God with a contingency plan in the background, we will never know the true rewards of answered prayer.

Once, when I was sick, I kept telling the Lord to heal me. The more I prayed, the worse the pain became. I took medication to mitigate my suffering, but it did not help. Finally, I came to the end of myself, and I began to pray earnestly. The Lord told me to speak to the pain and command it to go. At this point, I was angry with the enemy. I told the pain, "Go, in Jesus' name!" After an intense time of prayer and intercession, the pain began to subside. The moment I got serious in prayer was the moment things begin to shift.

The Spirit and Power of Elijah

In the gospel of Luke, the Bible gives a very interesting prophetic word concerning John the Baptist:

> *And he shall go before him in the spirit and power of Elias [Elijah], to turn the hearts of the fathers to the children, and the disobedient to the wisdom of the just; to make ready a people prepared for the Lord.*
>
> (Luke 1:17)

What is *"the spirit and power of Elias [Elijah]"*? We know that this Scripture was speaking specifically about John the Baptist, but there are elements that also apply to the church. Elijah was a man who possessed governmental authority. He challenged the religious system of Baal, which was very prevalent in his time, and called down fire from heaven and defeated Baal's prophets. (See 1 Kings 18.)

I believe it is time for the church to take up the prophetic mantle of Elijah and assume a position of authority over the powers of darkness that are hovering over our cities, communities, schools, and homes. Like Elijah did, we can tear down demonic infrastructures from within our prayer closets and release a spirit of revival and awakening in the land. In fact, we have received a greater anointing than Elijah because we have Christ living within us. You, too, can call down power from heaven.

Every time we pray, we engage in prophetic activity. We have been charged with calling forth God's will into manifestation. God has raised us up, as He did the prophet Elijah, to effect change in the world around us. What if you were the only one standing between the devil and your family? We have a tremendous responsibility to adopt God's heart for prayer in these last days.

THE SPIRIT OF PROPHECY IS RELEASED EVERY TIME WE ENGAGE IN EARNEST PRAYER AND INTERCESSION.

The second aspect of *"the spirit and power of Elias* [Elijah]*"* is that it will *"turn the hearts of the fathers to the children, and the disobedient to the wisdom of the just; to make ready a people prepared for the Lord"* (Luke 1:17). Many depictions of the end times cast it as a period of gloom and doom, but God has a beautiful plan of redemption in place. He desires to see families restored, communities healed, and people groups united. He wants those who are disobedient to turn to wisdom. And this vision is the ethos of our prophetic assignment in prayer.

I mentioned earlier that many years ago, my wife and I began a prayer service in our home. There were times when we would literally pray all night long; this was always a very powerful experience. It was during this period that the Lord began to unfold to us His plan for the ministry we are engaged in today. One night, while we were praying over our city, a woman joined us. She had undergone extensive surgery following a car accident and had metal rods throughout her body. As we were worshipping and praying, the fire of God fell on her, and she began to scream. Her wailing went on for nearly thirty minutes. After she finally got up from the floor, she quietly left. A few days later, I saw this same woman at a Christian bookstore. She testified that the metal rods in her legs had turned to bone, and she was able to walk and run without any pain. Hallelujah! This is a testament to what the fire of God can do. It is time for you to call down the fire of God to consume everything in your life that is not like Him, including sickness, disease, infirmity, fear, and despair. Our God is an all-consuming fire!

Prayer Gives Power and Influence

As I've said before, a praying person is a powerful person. If you want to gauge your level of power and influence in the earth, simply look at your prayer life. Jesus modeled this truth in His daily life on the earth. In the book of Matthew, the Bible says of Jesus, *"When he was come down from the mountain, great multitudes followed him"* (Matthew 8:1). What was Jesus doing on the mountain? He was praying! Notice that when He came down after praying, multitudes began to follow Him. Why? Prayer imparts influence! The more we pray, the more influence we have over situations, circumstances, and others' lives. Through prayer, we have capacity to affect the character, development, and behavior of people and events. The word "influence" is derived from the Latin word *influenza*, which is an infectious virus. When we are constantly praying in earnest, we become "infectious" with the kingdom of God.

I have experienced this phenomenon firsthand. During college, I had several peculiar experiences. I was in class one day when a young lady I didn't know got up from her seat, grabbed me by the hand, and pulled me outside the classroom door. I was almost certain she was trying to flirt with me, so you can imagine my surprise when she said, "I know I don't know you, but I'm going through a very difficult time, and I need you to pray for me!" I think I was shocked, flattered, and disappointed, all at the same time. (She was a very beautiful young lady, after all.) Seeing her eyes well up with tears, I began to pray for her. When I was done, she thanked me, and we never spoke to each other again. Why did she ask me to pray for her? What was it about me that drew her toward me? I believe it was the "influence" of the Holy Spirit.

THERE ARE PEOPLE AROUND YOU WHO ARE DESPERATELY DEPENDENT UPON YOUR PRAYER LIFE.

On another occasion, I was walking down the campus's main sidewalk when a young man came up to me and said, "Excuse me, sir—can I pray with you? The Lord told me that you are a man of God, and I wanted to know if I could pray with you." Even though I was not in the mood to pray with anyone, I had been taught to never refuse prayer, so I reluctantly obliged. He took me by the hand, and I closed my eyes as he began to pray for me. While we were praying, I felt another hand—a crusty one—grab mine. I didn't want to look up, so I kept my eyes shut. When the prayer concluded, I opened my eyes and saw the second person who had grabbed my hand—a homeless man who happened to be walking by while we were praying. He told us that he was drawn to us because he felt the presence of God. After speaking with him for several moments, we led him in a prayer of salvation. Hallelujah!

Prayer is more powerful than we could ever imagine. Again, when we pray, we are inviting the presence and power of God to manifest in and through us. We become conduits of supernatural encounters with God. We become supernatural influences in our homes, workplaces, neighborhoods, and schools. We become a part of the Elijah generation—a generation of prophetic prayer warriors who dare to release God's kingdom influence in the earth.

God Is Redefining Prayer

For too many years, prayer has been viewed as an extremely inconvenient chore or a necessary evil. That mind-set *must* change. Some people have a negative view of prayer as a result of hurts, disappointments, and trauma they have experienced. They feel that God has not answered them in the past, so why even bother praying to Him in the future? This is a very dangerous mind-set! Others have a subconscious aversion to prayer.

Regardless of our experiences, a biblical perspective on prayer will enable us to reap its vast benefits. As we've seen, the book of James exhorts us to pray as the prophet Elijah did. So, let's take another look at Elijah's prayer:

> *And Elijah the Tishbite, who was of the inhabitants of Gilead, said unto Ahab, As the* Lord *God of Israel liveth, before whom I stand, there shall not be dew nor rain these years, but according to my word.* (1 Kings 17:1)

The irony of James' remark is that Elijah's "prayer" isn't a prayer at all! At least, not in the conventional sense of the word. The only thing Elijah did was make a prophetic declaration that it would not rain on the earth. He didn't beg God to stop the rain; he didn't use a bunch of eloquent words; he did not follow a religious formula. He simply made a faith-filled, prophetic declaration. Either James misunderstood the account of Elijah, or God is redefining prayer. I don't know about you, but I think the latter is more likely. Beyond praying prayers of mere supplication and thanksgiving, we must tap into the mind of God and speak forth His purposes in the earth.

PRAYER IS MORE THAN A RELIGIOUS
RESPONSIBILITY; IT IS A PROPHETIC ACT BASED
ON FAITH IN THE POWER OF GOD.

Someone once asked the famous evangelist Smith Wigglesworth whether he prayed for long periods of time. He responded, "I never pray for more than fifteen minutes at a time, but I never go more than fifteen minutes without praying." In other words, he lived a life of continual prayer and intercession. God is calling all of us to live such a life.

How much time do you think Elijah had to spend praying over the heavens before he saw results? Don't get me wrong; I believe in persistence and perseverance in prayer. But I think it is equally important for us to believe what we are saying when we pray. From now on, we will see results from our prayer lives because we have had a revelation of the purpose and power of prayer. Remember, everything in the kingdom of God is based on revelation.

Revelation is the catalyst for change and manifestation. Jesus always spoke with confidence because He was thoroughly convinced that the Father *always* heard Him. For example, in the gospel of John, Jesus told the man at the pool of Bethesda, *"Rise, take up thy bed, and walk"* (John 5:8). Jesus spoke with faith, boldness, and authority, knowing that what He said would surely come to pass. He never doubted for a second! Is it possible for you and me to pray this way? According to John 14:12, it is!

You and I can declare with the boldness of Elijah that change will come to our families, our churches, and our cities. We can close doors on the enemy through the power of prayer. The key is to pray with every fiber of our being, knowing that God's Word can never fail.

What Spirit Are You Of?

There is a practice in the church of employing ungodly practices to control others, under the guise of spirituality. Known as "charismatic witchcraft," this tactic may include attempting to use one's prayers to control the will of another person. God does not sanction this practice. He has given all His children free will, meaning we have the ability, as free moral agents, to make our own choices. It is healthy and encouraged to give and receive sound counsel or to pray that people will make the right decisions (based on God's Word). However, there is a stark difference between godly influence and manipulation. Using prayer to control your spouse, your children, or your fellow church members is not of God.

192 *The Power of Prophetic Prayer*

Another form of charismatic witchcraft is praying judgment or calamity over people. There is a place for prayers of imprecation when asking for God's justice to prevail in a given situation (for example, in cases of child abuse or sex trafficking). But this is much different from seeking personal vindication against someone who refuses to do what we want or disagrees with our vantage point. I once prayed for a woman who had been cursed by her pastor. He had told her that if she left the church, she would never conceive children. This is demonic! Yet there are many people in the body of Christ who have fallen victim to this type of activity. As a pastor, I can tell you that those in spiritual leadership should *never* seek to manipulate or control others. I am continually praying for people and offering them counsel, but there comes a time when I must step back and let them make their own decisions.

PRAYER SHOULD NEVER BE A TOOL FOR MANIPULATION AND CONTROL BUT RATHER A MEANS OF INFLUENCING THE EARTH WITH THE CULTURE OF HEAVEN.

I have heard of people praying for bad things to happen to their enemies, justifying themselves with Psalm 105:15—in which God says, *"Touch not mine anointed, and do my prophets no harm."* However, these people rip this verse out of its biblical context. It was referring to a specific situation in the Old Testament that was forever changed by the arrival of Christ. Luke chapter 9 demonstrates just how much the incarnation of the Son of Man altered things:

> And it came to pass, when the time was come that he should be received up, he stedfastly set his face to go to Jerusalem, and sent messengers before his face: and they went, and entered into a village of the Samaritans, to make ready for him. And they did not receive him, because his

face was as though he would go to Jerusalem. And when his disciples
James and John saw this, they said, Lord, wilt thou that we command
fire to come down from heaven, and consume them, even as Elias did?
But he turned, and rebuked them, and said, Ye know not what manner
of spirit ye are of. For the Son of man is not come to destroy men's lives,
but to save them.   (Luke 9:51–56)

When the Samaritans wronged Jesus, the disciples thought it would
be fitting to ask God to send fire down to destroy them. To this suggestion,
Jesus responded, *"Ye know not what manner of spirit ye are of. For the Son of*
man is not come to destroy men's lives, but to save them." We must remember
that the heart of Jesus is healing, restoration, and salvation. If these elements are not at the core of our prayer culture, then we are operating in the
wrong spirit. Jesus is the express image of the Father (see Hebrews 1:2–3),
and His actions demonstrate the essence of the new covenant. Jesus never
cursed people. He never gave anyone cancer or leprosy. If Jesus didn't curse
people, then neither should we. Our prayers should always be used as a
means of building up God's people and advancing His kingdom, not tear-
ing people down. No matter what others may have done to harm us, we
must make sure we are praying in the right spirit.

Prophetic Utterances

Earlier, we saw that Elijah made a decree that it would not rain in
Israel for three and a half years. God honored Elijah's request and shut the
heavens. The Bible tells us in James 5 that we can get the same results if
we pray effectually and fervently. I am convinced that because Elijah was
a prophet, his prayer was actually a prophetic utterance—an act of saying
or expressing something under the inspiration of the Holy Spirit. When
Elijah made the declaration about the rain, he was not speaking of his own
accord but was speaking under divine inspiration.

One night, while praying, I felt something come over me. I began to
speak things into the atmosphere concerning our church and city. I didn't
realize it at the time, but I was releasing prophetic utterances by the Holy
Spirit. When we pray, we must be sensitive to what the Holy Spirit is saying.

He desires to use our mouths to release things into the atmosphere, as He did at Pentecost: *"And they* [the disciples] *were all filled with the Holy Spirit, and began to speak with other tongues, as the Spirit gave them **utterance**"* (Acts 2:4). The word *"utterance"* here comes from the Greek word *apophtheggomai,* which means "to speak forth dignified and elevated discourse." Notice that the disciples did the speaking, and the Holy Spirit gave the utterance.

THE HOLY SPIRIT DESIRES TO RELEASE DIVINE UTTERANCES THROUGH BELIEVERS WHEN THEY PRAY.

The purpose of prophetic utterances is to build up our faith and bring us comfort. As the apostle Paul instructs us,

> *For he that speaketh in an unknown tongue speaketh not unto men, but unto God: for no man understandeth him; howbeit in the spirit he speaketh mysteries. But he that prophesieth speaketh unto men to edification, and exhortation, and comfort.* (1 Corinthians 14:2–3)

When the Bible says that prophecy brings edification, exhortation, and comfort *"unto men,"* it means these things are brought to you, too.

King David is an example of a famous Bible character who was encouraged by prophetic utterances:

> *And it came to pass, when David and his men were come to Ziklag on the third day, that the Amalekites had invaded the south, and Ziklag, and smitten Ziklag, and burned it with fire; and had taken the women captives, that were therein: they slew not any, either great or small, but carried them away, and went on their way. So David and his men came to the city, and, behold, it was burned with fire; and their wives, and their sons, and their daughters, were taken captives. Then David and the people that were with him lifted up their voice and wept, until*

they had no more power to weep. And David's two wives were taken captives, Ahinoam the Jezreelitess, and Abigail the wife of Nabal the Carmelite. And David was greatly distressed; for the people spake of stoning him, because the soul of all the people was grieved, every man for his sons and for his daughters: but David encouraged himself in the LORD *his God. And David said to Abiathar the priest, Ahimelech's son, I pray thee, bring me hither the ephod. And Abiathar brought thither the ephod to David. And David enquired at the* LORD, *saying, Shall I pursue after this troop? shall I overtake them? And he answered him, Pursue: for thou shalt surely overtake them, and without fail recover all.*　　　　　　　　　　　　　　　　　　(1 Samuel 30:1–8)

David was in a very desperate situation. It looked as if everything around him was falling apart. His wives had been kidnapped, and the entire camp had been burned. The people were ready to stone him. Look again at David's response in his great distress: He *"encouraged himself in the* LORD.*"* There will be times when we have to encourage ourselves while everything seems to be falling apart. David had enough prophetic foresight to seek the Lord. David asked Abiathar the priest to bring him the ephod—a ceremonial garment worn by the priests—and then he asked the Lord for divine direction about whether to pursue his enemies. The Lord spoke to him and said, *"Pursue: for thou shalt surely overtake them, and without fail recover all."* I don't believe this was some dramatic public display of prayer but rather a very private supplication. David took upon himself the mantle of intercession and thereby received a prophetic word of encouragement from God. And when he acted on that word, he enacted a supernatural breakthrough. In the same manner, God wants to speak prophetically to you and me. He wants to release a prophetic utterance that will shift the circumstances in our lives. I declare that you are about to "pursue and recover" everything that the enemy has stolen from you.

The Ministry of Reconciliation

As new covenant believers in the Messiah, you and I have received the ministry of reconciliation: *"And all things are of God, who hath reconciled us to himself by Jesus Christ, and hath given to us the **ministry of reconciliation**"* (2 Corinthians 5:18). The term for *"reconciliation"* here is Greek word *katallagē*, which means "exchanging equivalent values." Simply put, you and I have received a supernatural ministry that enables us to reconcile the people around us back to God through the exchange of values. Every action we commit is a result of our value system. When we pray for people, we are actually inviting the Holy Spirit to change their value system. The ministry of prophetic prayer is a ministry of reconciliation, not a ministry of destruction. We are called to pray for God to deliver the sinner, not to bring judgment upon the sinner. In the natural world, when you reconcile an account, you must balance out that which is written on the income statement with the assets that are actually housed in inventory. In the same way, we have been called to reconcile the culture of heaven with the reality of the earthly realm until the two become balanced.

ANY SITUATION CAN BE RECONCILED IF YOU ARE WILLING TO PRAY AND RECEIVE GOD'S DIVINE SOLUTION.

The truth is, we live in a very broken world. People are hurting. Many are battling despair and hopelessness. There is a widespread need to encounter the power and presence of God like never before. What if I told you that you hold the key to reformation and revival? What if I told you that you have the power to effect change in the lives of those around you? As a minister of reconciliation, you have been called by God to release the kingdom everywhere you go. Nothing is more instrumental in restoring people back to God than prayer. Let's pray earnestly for our loved ones. Let's pray for our churches and schools. Let's pray for our community, our city, our world.

Prophetic Prayer

Father, I thank You that You hear prayer; it's because of Your power that my fervent prayer will accomplish much! You bend

Your ear to listen to my cry; You give me the spirit and power of Elijah. What I say according to Your Word will happen, because Your Word cannot return to You void. I declare that my prayers never manipulate or control others. Instead, my words bring the culture of heaven down to earth! My words and my life are hope and peace to the people around me. Reconcile this world to You, Lord! I call down Your power to destroy the darkness around me. Your kingdom come, Your will be done, in the matchless name of Jesus, amen!

Prophetic Insights

1. Is it OK to have a contingency plan in the works, in case your prayer isn't answered?

2. What can we learn from Elijah's prayer in 1 Kings 17?

3. How can you manifest a "ministry of reconciliation"?

15

Releasing Your Destiny Through Intercession

*And we know that **all things work together for good** to them that
love God, to them who are the called according to his purpose. For
whom he did foreknow, he also did predestinate to be conformed
to the image of his Son, that he might be the firstborn among many
brethren. Moreover whom he did predestinate, them he also called:
and whom he called, them he also justified: and whom he justified,
them he also glorified.*
—Romans 8:28–30

hus far, we have examined the profound power of prayer in the life of
the believer. We have also seen that prayer allows us to tap into the prophetic dimension of our born-again nature. How amazing is this? Every
day, people all over the world face difficult situations and traumatic experiences. You yourself may be going through a trial right now. But no matter
where you are or what you are going through, prayer can change things in
your life. God is the righteous Judge who desires to bring His justice and
restoration in every situation we face.

Years ago, I discovered firsthand that prayer was more than a religious
activity. I realized that prayer had the power to alter the course of my life.

200 The Power of Prophetic Prayer

Everyone in the world today is looking for his or her purpose. People everywhere are asking, "What is my destiny, and how do I fulfill it?" Is there a connection between your individual destiny and your prayer life? I believe that prayer is the key to unlocking your destiny! It has been debated for years in the body of Christ whether the destiny of individuals is fixed (independent of their actions) or if it can be altered by their choices and actions. But let me just ask you: if everything that happens is bound to happen, regardless of our actions, then why did God tell us to pray in the first place? The very existence of the act of prayer implies that you and I can affect what happens in the future.

PRAYER HAS THE SUPERNATURAL POWER TO CHANGE THE COURSE OF OUR DESTINY.

One of the most powerful displays of faith, courage, and perseverance in prayer that I have ever read is recorded in the book of Isaiah. *"In those days was Hezekiah sick unto death. And Isaiah the prophet the son of Amoz came unto him, and said unto him, Thus saith the LORD, Set thine house in order: for thou shalt die, and not live"* (Isaiah 38:1). Notice that the prophet Isaiah spoke the word of the Lord to Hezekiah. This was a sovereign utterance from God: *"For thou shalt die, and not live."* The king's reaction was much different from what most of us would have anticipated. Instead of complaining, getting angry at the prophet, or becoming bitter, Hezekiah prayed.

Then Hezekiah turned his face toward the wall, and prayed unto the LORD, and said, Remember now, O LORD, I beseech thee, how I have walked before thee in truth and with a perfect heart, and have done that which is good in thy sight. And Hezekiah wept sore. Then came the word of the LORD to Isaiah, saying, Go, and say to Hezekiah, Thus saith the LORD, the God of David thy father, I have heard thy prayer, I have seen thy tears: behold, I will add unto thy days fifteen years.

(Isaiah 38:2–5)

King Hezekiah prayed to the Lord and asked Him to remember His covenant. As a result of his prayer, King Hezekiah had fifteen years added to his life! The moral of the story is further proof of what we learned from James: heartfelt, sincere prayer has the power to change your life.

The Sincere Prayer of the Righteous

In our discussion of the power of effectual, fervent prayer, we noted that Elijah prayed that it would not rain for a specific time period, and that God honored his request. We also discussed how God is no respecter of persons (see Acts 10:34)—you and I have the same ability as Elijah, if not an even greater ability than he. There is no doubt that you and I can receive answered prayer every time. The key is our sincerity! The motivation of our hearts needs to be free from pretense, deceit, and hypocrisy. Contrary to popular opinion, God considers our motives of equal importance to our actions. The Bible says, *"Keep thy heart with all diligence; for out of it are the issues of life"* (Proverbs 4:23). The word *"issues"* here literally means "source." The heart is the repository of our inner thoughts, longings, and affections. It is the source of everything we think about and act upon; therefore, the heart is key when it comes to prayer. Prayer is not magic! Prayer is the sincere activity of a heart surrendered to God. The more we surrender our hearts to the Lord, the more sincere we will be, and the more powerful our prayer lives will become. Unfortunately, we live in a society filled with pretense. We are often encouraged to focus on the exterior, while the interior is neglected. Beloved, we must allow the Holy Spirit to search our hearts, that we might make sure there is no deceit, pretense, or hypocrisy within. Remember, the Bible says, *"For with the heart man believeth unto righteousness; and with the mouth confession is made unto salvation"* (Romans 10:10). We must have faith in order to receive answered prayer, and faith comes from the heart.

PROPHETIC PRAYER IS ONLY AS EFFECTIVE AS
THE LEVEL OF OUR SINCERITY AND FAITH.

This is why the condition of our hearts is of utmost importance to God. Most people are not fully aware of the state of their hearts. And many people, even within in the body of Christ, have a "divided heart"; thus, they find it difficult to pray and to receive answers from God. Jesus admonished us: "**No man can serve two masters**: *for either he will hate the one, and love the other; or else he will hold to the one, and despise the other. Ye cannot serve God and mammon*" (Matthew 6:24). We cannot be fully committed to God's purposes for our lives if we are simultaneously serving our own interests or selfish ambitions.

There have been times in the past when I have prayed for a particular outcome, meanwhile expecting something totally different to happen. These were instances of spiritual insanity! In the same way, many people pray for healing in their bodies, but they are enjoying the benefits of being sick, such as being waited on and having an excuse to stay home from work. Such individuals are praying with a divided heart—a condition that the apostle James warned us about:

> But let him ask [pray] *in faith, nothing wavering. For he that wavereth is like a wave of the sea driven with the wind and tossed. For let not that man think that he shall receive any thing of the Lord. A double minded man is unstable in all his ways.* (James 1:6–8)

Notice that this passage uses the term "double minded." People who are double-minded pray with divided interests. They have not resolved in their hearts what they really desire from God.

Once we have embraced God's purposes with all our heart, we can pray with all our heart. Beloved, there is no "plan B" in prayer! There is no contingency plan. Either we believe God completely and implicitly, or we believe Him not at all! This is why it is important that we allow the Word of God to permeate our hearts and produce in us the fruit of sincerity and truth. Today, I want you to ask God to search your heart and expose any insincerity that may be undermining your prayer life.

Overcoming Destiny Stagnation

Ever since I was born again, I have experienced many things that threatened to hinder me from walking in my God-given destiny. The Christian life is not static; rather, we're supposed to be constantly moving forward, ever perceiving more and more of God's glory: *"But we all, with open face beholding as in a glass the glory of the Lord, are changed into the same image from **glory to glory**, even as by the Spirit of the Lord"* (2 Corinthians 3:18). All believers should experience a fresh manifestation of the glory of God every day.

We are like travelers on a train, moving toward Christ; as long as we remain on the train, we will arrive at our destination. This is the way our destinies have been crafted by God, and He is the One who keeps our train on the tracks, *"having **predestinated** us unto the adoption of children by Jesus Christ to himself, according to the good pleasure of his will"* (Ephesians 1:5).

Earlier, we alluded to the predestination debate, which asks, "Is our destiny fixed, with no chance of alteration? Or do we have a say in what happens in our lives?" Well, contrary to popular opinion, all of us *have* been predestined, with destinies that have been predetermined, or decided beforehand, by God. In other words, God has already decided on His plan and purpose for your life. He has predetermined the end goal of every believer. And what is that end goal? The apostle Paul told us plainly: *"The adoption of children by Jesus Christ to himself, according to the good pleasure of his will"* (Ephesians 1:5). Paul adds in the book of Romans, *"For whom he did foreknow, he also did predestinate to be **conformed** to the image of his Son, that he might be the firstborn among many brethren"* (Romans 8:29). In other words, the final destination of every born-again believer is to look like Jesus, to think like Jesus, and to be like Jesus.

GOD HAS A PURPOSE FOR OUR LIVES, AND THE MORE WE COMMIT OURSELVES TO PRAYER, THE MORE WE TAP INTO HIS DIVINE PURPOSE.

We see an Old Testament parallel to this New Testament truth in the following famous passage from Jeremiah:

For I know the thoughts that I think toward you, saith the LORD, *thoughts of peace, and not of evil, to give you an expected end. Then shall ye call upon me, and ye shall go and pray unto me, and I will hearken unto you. And ye shall seek me, and find me, when ye shall search for me with all your heart.*   (Jeremiah 29:11–13)

God told the prophet Jeremiah, and the Israelites, that He had a plan for them. Despite all the challenges and difficulties they were experiencing at the time, God had ordained an *"expected end"* for them. This expected end was good and not evil! The same is true for us today. God desires to prosper, heal, deliver, restore, and bless us in every area. This is our purpose! Although we all have varying assignments to fulfill within the body of Christ, we have the same corporate purpose. One thing we can be sure of is that God's purposes for our lives are *good*.

The moment we were born again, we caught a ride on God's destiny train; and ever since then, the enemy of our souls has sought to do everything in his power to throw you and me off the tracks. The enemy knows that the purposes of God for us are awesome and are for the advancement of the very kingdom that the devil hates; therefore, he always attempts to halt our progress. This is what I call "destiny stagnation."

God told the Israelites that they would go into captivity for seventy years, and that afterward He would bring them out and prosper them. This was a prophetic word from God. Remember, prophetic words are not fulfilled automatically; when we receive them, we must stay in faith and prayer to see them manifest! What has God promised you? Are you willing to place a demand on it by faith? Are you willing to pray without ceasing until it comes to pass? It wasn't until the prophet Daniel experienced an epiphany that the Israelites realized the time of their captivity had passed, because up to then they were in a state of spiritual stagnation. How did they break out of this state of spiritual impotence and stagnation? The key was prayer—prophetic prayer, to be exact!

In the first year of [King Darius'] reign I Daniel understood by books the number of the years, whereof the word of the LORD *came to Jeremiah the prophet, that he would accomplish seventy years in the desolations of Jerusalem. And I set my face unto the Lord God, to seek by prayer and supplications, with fasting, and sackcloth, and ashes: And I prayed unto the* LORD *my God, and made my confession, and said, O Lord, the great and dreadful God, keeping the covenant and mercy to them that love him, and to them that keep his commandments.*   (Daniel 9:2–4)

The prophet Daniel had a revelation that something was amiss. He noticed that the people of Israel were outside the plan of God for their lives. Daniel saw in the scrolls that their time of captivity had long expired. As a result of this revelation, he entered into a time of prayer and fasting.

THE WORD OF GOD REVEALS OUR DESTINIES AND ACTS AS THE DIVINE LOCATION COORDINATES OF HEAVEN.

To walk in our God-given destinies, we first must have a revelation from the Word of God. We must understand that the Word of God is the ultimate will of God for our lives. The Word of God always determines where we are and where we are destined to be; so, if we want to know where we are supposed to be, our first step should be to consult the Word of God.

Once the Word of God has revealed our position, the next step is to engage in earnest prayer. This is exactly what Daniel did! I want you to imagine a sort of spiritual Global Positioning System (GPS). The purpose of this spiritual GPS is to transmit your location via satellite and to provide you with directions to the place where God intends for you to be. Prayer is our heavenly GPS, and the Word of God provides the coordinates and instructions to enable us to reach our destination.

Destiny-Accelerating Prayer

In the book of Daniel, we have a very telling picture of the profound power of prayer to bring change and to alter the course of our destinies.

What would have happened if Daniel hadn't had the courage, faith, and foresight to pray? It is quite possible that nothing would have changed in his life, or in the lives of millions of others, for that matter. Daniel engaged in what I like to call "destiny-accelerating prayer"—prayer that literally accelerates personal destinies. And I believe that we can pray in the same way.

Think of the process of jump-starting a stalled engine. To get the engine going, you have to add power. Every time we pray in faith from a pure heart, we are supernaturally jump-starting our destinies. Daniel prayed this way! I want to share the following portion of Daniel's prayer. It may seem long-winded and rambling, but it contains a key component that I believe will bless your life:

> **We have sinned**, *and have committed iniquity, and have done wickedly, and have rebelled, even by departing from thy precepts and from thy judgments:* **neither have we hearkened unto thy servants the prophets**, *which spake in thy name to our kings, our princes, and our fathers, and to all the people of the land.* **O Lord, righteousness belongeth unto thee, but unto us confusion of faces**, *as at this day; to the men of Judah, and to the inhabitants of Jerusalem, and unto all Israel, that are near, and that are far off, through all the countries whither thou hast driven them, because of their trespass that they have trespassed against thee. O Lord, to us belongeth confusion of face, to our kings, to our princes, and to our fathers, because we have sinned against thee.* **To the Lord our God belong mercies and forgivenesses, though we have rebelled against him;** *neither have we obeyed the voice of the* Lord *our God, to walk in his laws, which he set before us by his servants the prophets. Yea, all Israel have transgressed thy law, even by departing, that they might not obey thy voice; therefore the curse is poured upon us, and the oath that is written in the law of Moses the servant of God, because we have sinned against him. And he hath confirmed his words, which he spake against us, and against our judges that judged us, by bringing upon us a great evil: for under the whole heaven hath not been done as hath been done upon Jerusalem. As it is written in the law of Moses, all this evil is come upon us: yet made we not our prayer before the* Lord *our God, that we might turn from our iniquities, and understand thy truth. Therefore hath the* Lord *watched upon the evil, and brought it upon us:*

for the LORD *our God is righteous in all his works which he doeth: for we obeyed not his voice. And now, O Lord our God, that hast brought thy people forth out of the land of Egypt with a mighty hand, and hast gotten thee renown, as at this day; we have sinned, we have done wickedly.* **O** LORD, **according to all thy righteousness, I beseech thee, let thine anger and thy fury be turned away** *from thy city Jerusalem, thy holy mountain: because for our sins, and for the iniquities of our fathers, Jerusalem and thy people are become a reproach to all that are about us. Now therefore,* **O our God, hear the prayer of thy servant,** *and his supplications, and cause thy face to shine upon thy sanctuary that is desolate, for the Lord's sake. O my God, incline thine ear, and hear; open thine eyes, and behold our desolations, and the city which is called by thy name: for we do not present our supplications before thee for our righteousnesses, but for thy great mercies.* **O Lord, hear; O Lord, forgive;** *O Lord, hearken and do; defer not, for thine own sake, O my God: for thy city and thy people are called by thy name.* (Daniel 9:5–19)

When you hear the term "destiny-accelerating prayer," you might think of a prayer that commands God to act, declares the might of one's faith, and exults in one's God-given powers. But how did Daniel begin his destiny-accelerating prayer? *With repentance.* The prophet Daniel began by acknowledging that the Israelites had sinned against God. Daniel was acting as a prophetic intercessor on behalf of Israel. He humbled himself and repented on behalf of the entire nation.

You and I can benefit greatly from praying prayers of repentance. I am not suggesting that we be legalistic, but I am saying that God looks at our hearts. Prayers of repentance simply acknowledge wrongdoing on our part. The more frequently we admit our shortcomings and failures in prayer, the more powerful our prayers will become. Repentance cleanses the heart and removes blockages that would hinder our prayer lives. We are admonished in Scripture to confess our faults. (See, for example, James 5:16.) Prayers of repentance have the power to accelerate our destinies!

What would happen in our nation if we saints fell on our knees and repented of the part we have played in the condition of our country? I believe that our nation would realize her manifest destiny!

The second thing that Daniel did was remind God of His covenant. Remember, God is a covenantal God. He responds to covenants! The moment we acknowledge God's covenant in prayer, something shifts in the spiritual realm.

Breaking the Spirit of Destiny Abortion

Through heartfelt intercession and sincere repentance, Daniel broke the spirit of destiny abortion hovering over Israel. I decree and declare that every spirit of destiny abortion in your life is broken. I declare in Jesus' name that whatever tactics Satan would use to stagnate, undermine, or abort your destiny and keep you from coming into the purpose and plan of God for your life are broken right now!

Once you learn how to identify destiny-aborting spirits, you can easily break their power from your life. They often manifest themselves in the following ways:

Pride

The Bible is very clear about the danger of pride. When we are operating in pride, we run the serious risk of prematurely aborting our destinies. The Bible admonishes us against pride, saying, *"Pride goeth before destruction, and an haughty spirit before a fall"* (Proverbs 16:18). Pride is defined as arrogance, haughtiness, or a vain concentration on oneself. Prideful people are incapable of true repentance; and we have seen the power of repentance to accelerate our destinies. The Hebrew word for *"destruction"* in Proverbs 16:18 is *sheber*, which means "breaking, fracture, crushing, breach, crash, ruin, and shattering." Those who walk in pride and an exaggerated sense of self-importance stand the risk of shattering, crushing, and breaching their own destinies. If there is any form of pride operating in our hearts, we must repent of it immediately and ask the Holy Spirit to cleanse us and to teach us to walk in humility.

Rebellion

One of the most dangerous spirits in the body of Christ is rebellion, or any act of open resistance. The Bible says, *"For rebellion is as the **sin of witchcraft**,* *and stubbornness is as iniquity and idolatry"* (1 Samuel 15:23). The Bible equates rebellion with witchcraft because the rebel is always attempting to manipulate God's Word and will to fit his or her own will and desires. Rebels refuse to submit to God and to any God-ordained authority over their lives. Those who operate in a spirit of rebellion tend to refuse to obey God, and they incite the same disobedience in others. They generally lack a vital prayer life, because sincere prayer requires submission to God. The truth is, all of us have a tendency to walk in rebellion, at times. We must ask the Lord to uproot any spirit of rebellion in our hearts so that we may receive His gracious plans for our lives.

Bitterness

Many people in the body of Christ are harboring bitterness, resentment, and unforgiveness in their hearts, little knowing that these attitudes are not only hindering their prayers but also quite possibly aborting their destinies. Many years ago, I went through a very traumatic experience in ministry that caused me to become bitter. I didn't even realize that I was bitter until the Lord exposed this sinful heart attitude to me. The Bible says, *"[Look] diligently lest any man fail of the grace of God; lest any root of bitterness springing up trouble you, and thereby **many be defiled"*** (Hebrews 12:15). When someone offends, hurts, mistreats, or otherwise wrongs us, it is critical that we forgive and release that person immediately. If we refuse to forgive our offender, the offense is likely to become a bitter root in our hearts that will contaminate our prayers, damage our faith walks, and ultimately keep us from fulfilling God's plans for our lives. I don't know about you, but there is no offense that I would consider worth aborting the plan and purpose of God for my life. Let's make the decision today to forgive our offenders and to pray for our enemies.

THE ENEMY ATTEMPTS TO USE THE SPIRITS
OF PRIDE, REBELLION, AND BITTERNESS TO
DRAIN YOUR PRAYERS OF THEIR POWER AND
EFFECTIVENESS, AND ULTIMATELY TO DERAIL YOU
FROM THE TRACK TO YOUR DESTINY.

Fasting and Prayer: God's Nuclear Power

I think few spiritual disciplines have been more understated in terms of importance in our modern church culture than fasting and prayer. These disciplines, when practiced together, constitute one of the most powerful spiritual weapons available to the body of Christ today. I like to call fasting and prayer "God's nuclear power"! It is important to note that in conjunction with praying his "destiny-accelerating prayer," the prophet Daniel fasted for Israel:

> *And I set my face unto the Lord God, to seek by prayer and supplications, with fasting, and sackcloth, and ashes…. Yea, whiles I was speaking in prayer, even the man Gabriel, whom I had seen in the vision at the beginning, being caused to fly swiftly, touched me about the time of the evening oblation. And he informed me, and talked with me, and said, O Daniel, I am now come forth to give thee skill and understanding. At the beginning of thy supplications the commandment came forth, and I am come to shew thee; for thou art greatly beloved: therefore understand the matter, and consider the vision.* (Daniel 9:3, 21–23)

The moment Daniel began fasting and praying, something shifted supernaturally, and the angel of the Lord was revealed. We'll discuss angelic assistance in further detail later on; but, for now, try to imagine years of captivity being turned around in a single day. This is exactly what happened when Daniel prayed!

Jesus understood the power of fasting and prayer—it was a vital part of His earthly ministry. In Mark 9, Jesus' disciples were not successful at casting out a deaf and dumb spirit from a young boy. (See Mark 9:17–18.) Jesus rebuked the foul spirit (see verse 25), then explained to His disciples, "*This kind* [of spirit] *can come forth by nothing, but by prayer and fasting*" (Mark 9:29). I like the way Jesus' response is expressed in the *Amplified Bible*: "*This kind cannot be driven out by anything but prayer and fasting*" (Mark 9:29 AMP). The terms "drive out" or "expel" convey a sense of forcefulness. It makes me think of an atomic bomb exploding, thereby releasing a thermonuclear energy equivalent to thousands of sticks of dynamite. The power from a nuclear bomb is so great that it leaves behind a haze of radiation long after the blast is over. This is the power of fasting and prayer! When we combine our faith with prayer and fasting, we catalyze a supernatural reaction that produces an explosion of miracles, breakthroughs, and deliverances. Unfortunately, many people have never experienced the power of fasting and prayer. They assume that the practice is old-fashioned. I have even heard people suggest that fasting is no longer necessary because we are under grace. However, the apostle Paul, speaking from the standpoint of the new covenant, affirmed the necessity of fasting: *"But I keep under my body, and bring it into **subjection**: lest that by any means, when I have preached to others, I myself should be a castaway"* (1 Corinthians 9:27). The truth is that fasting is not for God; it is for us! By abstaining from physical food for a period of time, we position ourselves spiritually to hear clearly from God.

Releasing Angelic Assistance Through Intercession

We have seen the power of prayer to intervene in the course of our destinies, bringing about change and supernatural turnaround. If you are not excited yet, then perhaps you need to pinch yourself and make sure you are still awake! My earnest desire is for you to experience an epiphany in your perception of prayer. We are living in the most critical time in human history, and prayer is the catalyst for transformation in our world. I don't know about you, but I am not sitting back and waiting for Jesus to return before I make a difference on the earth.

In addition to prompting supernatural turnaround in our lives, prayer also has the ability to invite angelic assistance. The first appearance of angels in the Bible occurs in the book of Genesis:

> *And there came two angels to Sodom at even; and Lot sat in the gate of Sodom: and Lot seeing them rose up to meet them; and he bowed himself with his face toward the ground.* (Genesis 19:1)

The word for *"angels"* in this verse comes from the Hebrew word *mal'ak*, which, in almost every appearance in the Bible, means "messenger or representative." Angels are divine messengers of God, sent to perform a specific task or assignment. These beings vary in rank and power, but they all work as ministering spirits for the good of believers. In the book of Genesis, angels were sent to Lot to deliver him from judgment. These are what we would call angels of deliverance. Notice that these angels of deliverance were sent in direct response to Abraham's prayer of intercession, recorded in Genesis 18. Abraham stood in the gap between Lot and God's judgment of Sodom and Gomorrah. Through prayer, you and I can release angelic assistance in the earth.

We also see angels at work in the life of Daniel, preserving him from being mauled in the lions' den.

> *Then the king went to his palace, and passed the night fasting: neither were instruments of music brought before him: and his sleep went from him. Then the king arose very early in the morning, and went in haste unto the den of lions. And when he came to the den, he cried with a lamentable voice unto Daniel: and the king spake and said to Daniel, O Daniel, servant of the living God, is thy God, whom thou servest continually, able to deliver thee from the lions? Then said Daniel unto the king, O king, live for ever. My God hath sent his angel, and hath shut the lions' mouths, that they have not hurt me: forasmuch as before him innocency was found in me; and also before thee, O king, have I done no hurt.* (Daniel 6:18–22)

After making an irrevocable decree, the king fasted and prayed for Daniel, and God responded by sending an angel of divine protection to shut the mouths of the lions. Every time you and I make heartfelt intercession, we are imploring angelic assistance on behalf of others. Are your angels employed or unemployed? Earlier, we said that prayer and intercession have the power and ability to release divine solutions for our lives. Those divine solutions are sometimes accomplished by angels who minister to specific needs in the body of Christ. Even Jesus Himself received ministry from angels in response to prayer. (See, for example, Matthew 4:11.)

PROPHETIC PRAYER RELEASES ANGELIC ASSISTANCE INTO OUR LIVES. THE MORE WE PRAY, THE MORE ANGELS WE HAVE ON ASSIGNMENT.

Many years ago, I had entered into a season of severe spiritual stagnation and barrenness. I had no desire to pray, fast, or even read the Word. I felt stuck! I don't know if you have ever experienced a season such as this, but it is far from pleasant. One morning, I forced myself to my knees and cried out to God for help. The most amazing thing happened! I had an open vision of an angel standing behind me, pouring crystal spring water on my back. As soon as the water touched my back, I jumped up and began singing praises to the Lord. I was instantly filled with zeal and vitality. The season of spiritual barrenness was over! Hallelujah!

Then I looked up and saw a huge angelic being. The only thing that I could think to do was to ask his name. The angel responded, "My name is Joy." Glory to God! This is the power of prayer. I believe that angels of deliverance, breakthrough, healing, and protection are on their way to your location. Simply declare the Word of God out of your mouth: *"Bless the Lord, ye his angels, that excel in strength, that do his commandments, hearkening unto the voice of his word"* (Psalm 103:20).

Prayer of Divine Protection and Covering:

Father, in the name of Jesus Christ, I pray Your protection and covering over every person reading this book. We take authority over the spirits of darkness, destruction, calamity, fear, tragedy, murder, and death. We declare the supernatural protection of God to surround the people of God. We serve notice to every witch, warlock, and demon that this is the day the Lord has made. We declare that this day is God's day; may He alone be glorified. I pray that every child will come home safely and will experience no harm. May those seeking evil come to know Christ today! No weapon formed against us shall prosper. Keep Your people today from any hurt, harm, danger, hex, or curse. Today, evil shall not prevail, but we will overcome evil with good. Thank You, Lord, for being the shield and fortress of Your people. In Jesus' name, amen!

Your Destiny Awaits You!

I remember when DVDs first came out. They were a refreshing alternative to the often inconvenient VHS recording medium. As DVDs increased in popularity, their features became more advanced. Several years ago, it became relatively common for DVDs of popular films to be coded for alternate endings, so that viewers could choose which ending they wanted to see.

Like those DVDs, our lives have an alternate ending. Many times, the enemy tries to throw a wrench in our destinies. You may feel that your life is bound in a particular direction or destined for a specific ending, but prayer has the power to bring about an *alternate* ending. We saw that although the lives of both King Hezekiah and Daniel were bound for defeat because of the devil's machinations, God gave them both a different ending after they lifted their voices to Him in prayer. Through prayer, we can call forth the purposes of God and see them manifest in our lives. We don't have to settle for the ending the devil has in mind for ourselves or for our loved ones.

PRAYER OPENS OUR SPIRIT MAN TO OUR GOD-ORDAINED PURPOSE, PLAN, AND DESTINY.

We must exercise our spiritual responsibility to pray according to the will of God for our lives. Earlier, we discovered that the will of God is the Word of God. Once we discover what the Word of God says, it is time for us to pray the Word with all our heart. No matter the difficulties or challenges we are facing, the Word has the power to bring breakthrough. We must pray the Word! Prayer is the life force of the prophetic; therefore, we cannot release the mind of God without spending time in His presence. I can't tell you how many times I would have experienced a different outcome to a situation if I had only prayed rather than become preoccupied with my circumstances. The trick of the enemy is to get you and me to underestimate the profound power of prayer. Let us resolve not to fall for his trick!

Testimonies

I want to share a few testimonies from people who prayed prophetically and experienced alternate endings and altered destinies.

A young lady was devastated when a blood test indicated the presence of cancer in her body. She reached out via Facebook to our ministry for prayer, and we declared that her blood was completely healed, in Jesus' name. This is what she wrote:

> *Thank you for your prayers! All of my blood cells have normalized, and there is no cancer! Praise God who is my Healer!*

Another woman had been told by her doctors that she would never be able to conceive a child. In her desperation, she contacted us for prayer. We began agreeing in prayer that the curse over her womb was broken. We then cursed the barrenness and released the blessing, according to Exodus 26. We prophesied that she would conceive, in Jesus' name. Months later, we received notice that she was pregnant. Hallelujah!

Prayer has the power to shine light in your darkest hour. You are not waiting on your destiny to happen; your destiny is waiting on *you*! What are *you* waiting for? You hold the key to your future in your hands. The Bible says, *"For the earnest expectation of the creature waiteth for the manifestation of the sons of God"* (Romans 8:19). The Greek word for *"waiteth"* here is *apekdechomai*, which means "assiduously and patiently waiting for." The whole world is waiting in great anticipation and attentiveness for the manifestation of the children of God in the earth! That is your ultimate destiny—to be manifested as a son or daughter of the Most High.

Everything Is Working for Your Good

Romans 8:28 assures us, *"And we know that **all things** work together for good to them that love God, to them who are the called according to his purpose."*

God has the power to bring every part of your life together in such a way that His good plan is made manifest. However, the promise of Romans 8:28 is given exclusively to the intercessor: *"Likewise the Spirit also helpeth our infirmities: for we know not what we should pray for as we ought: but the Spirit itself maketh intercession for us with groanings which cannot be uttered"* (Romans 8:26). Prayer is the supernatural catalyst that brings the manifestation of our destinies. We are not victims! God hasn't called us to sit back and watch life happen but to partner with the Holy Spirit in prayer in order to see God's plan revealed. If we will commit ourselves to prayer and intercession, God will cause any situation to turn around for our good and His glory. Whatever the enemy means for our demise, God is working toward our good. But nothing in the kingdom of God happens by chance; we must apply prayer, faith, and obedience to every circumstance of our lives.

Seeing and Seizing Your Destiny

It has often been taught that we have no power over our future because our destinies are hidden from us. This may be a popular belief, but it is definitely not a biblical belief. It's understandable why people believe this when we look at 1 Corinthians 2:9: *"But as it is written, Eye hath not seen, nor ear heard, neither have entered into the heart of man, the things which God hath prepared for them that love him."* The average Christian reads this passage of Scripture and builds a theology around it. Without reading any further, they assume that this means "eyes have not seen what God has prepared for me, therefore I can never know what God is going to do!" In order to truly understand what the Bible actually said, however, we must read on: *"But God hath revealed them unto us by his Spirit: for the Spirit searcheth all things, yea, the deep things of God"* (verse 10). While it is truth that the mystery of our destinies may be hidden from our natural (or carnal) minds, it is the ardent desire of our heavenly Father to reveal hidden things of the future, by the Holy Spirit that dwells within us.

God has revealed the future. Now it is up to you to appropriate your destiny through the prayer of faith.

I want you to imagine for a moment that you are looking through a telescope. Now I want you to imagine that you could see your destiny through the lens of this telescope. What would you do? Remember, God's plans for you and me are good, peaceful, and prosperous! How would seeing your future change your present? Once you *see* your destiny, you will be in a position to *seize* your destiny. You can only seize that which you can see! The word *seize* means to take hold of something suddenly and forcibly. Jesus said in the Gospel of Matthew, "*And all things, whatsoever ye shall ask in prayer, believing, ye shall receive*" (Matthew 21:22.) The word "*receive*" here comes from the Greek word *lambanō*, which means "to take with the hand, lay hold of, any person or thing in order to use it." Does this sound familiar? Prayer is the telescope for our destiny, and God desires for every believer to see the purpose, plan, and destiny that He has ordained for us. Once we *see* this destiny in prayer, we must respond by *seizing* that which we see. Many people know how to use their faith when it comes to healing, finances, or the salvation of a loved one, but they have a tendency to neglect one of the most important aspects of our human experience: their destiny!

God's Wonderful Secret

When I was growing up, I was told that we should never question God. This was so deeply ingrained in my consciousness that I was afraid to ask God about anything. Often, I would want to understand why certain events took place in my life, but because of the belief system that I had about God, I would go to other sources to gain deeper insight. As you might have imagined, this always left me even more disappointed and frustrated. Unfortunately, religion and tradition can have an adverse effect on our spirituality. The truth was that God *wanted* to reveal things to me, but incorrect teaching was standing in my way. The Bible records that God desired to reveal the future to Abraham: "*And the LORD said, Shall I hide from Abraham that thing which I do; seeing that Abraham shall surely become a great and mighty nation, and all the nations of the earth shall be blessed in him?*" (Genesis 18:17–18). Similarly, God also desires a friendship with His children, the spiritual seed of Adam!

Earlier we talked about the fact that God is the revealer of secrets, but I want to take a moment and reemphasize the importance of viewing God the right way. God is not intimidated by your questions, nor will He punish you for your desire to know more. Maybe you have been wondering why a certain thing happened in your upbringing, or what the purpose of your life is. Regardless of what your questions are, God desires to answer them. You may not receive all the answers you want on this side of eternity, but God wants to dialogue with you. The platform for this dialogue is prayer! Ask and you shall receive, seek and you shall find, knock and the door will be opened. (See Matthew 7:7.) God's secret is that the answers you seek are just one prayer away!

Removing Hindrances to Your Destiny

Now that we have discovered that God's plan for you is good, and that He wants you to seize your future by faith, the next step is to pray! Below is a brief prayer that will address the obstacles to reaching your maximum potential in God, including obstacles like addiction and compulsive behavior:

Prayer to Break Addictions and Bring Deliverance

Father, in the name of Jesus Christ, I come to You boldly, yet also with humility and thanksgiving in my heart. I come to You now and recognize You as my Deliverer. You know exactly what I need. You know that which binds, torments, and defiles me. I believe that Jesus Christ is Your Son; He suffered on the cross and died, defeated Satan in hell, and was raised again on the third day. He now sits at Your right hand, praying for me, that I may have life, and have it in abundance. Lord Jesus, I surrender my life to You *now*!

I claim the promise of Your Word that *"whosoever shall call on the name of the Lord shall be saved"* (Acts 2:21). Deliver me and set me free, *now*! I loose myself from the devil and all his demonic agents, and command them to go from me now. I take authority over, and break the power of, the following: lust, perversion, addiction, unforgiveness, pornography, adultery, gossip, lying, idolatry, masturbation, fear, phobias, death, stealing, calamity, witchcraft, seducing spirits, suicide, depression, rejection, self-rejection, despair, double-mindedness, confusion, vanity, ego, addictive tendencies, and pride.

I expose my entire being to the blood of Jesus Christ and call upon the atoning sacrifice He made as payment for the penalty of my sin. I command any and all foul spirits to come out of me and leave me, now. Today is the day of my deliverance. Thank You for washing, cleansing, and making me free, in Jesus' name. Amen!

Prophetic Insights

1. What is the key to answered prayer?

2. What are the common signs of a destiny-aborting spirit?

3. If prayer is the life force of the prophetic, how can you super-charge the prophetic in your life?

PROPHETIC PRACTICUM

1. Pray a prayer that follows the Kingdom Protocol, as established in the Lord's Prayer (more accurately, "The Disciples' Prayer").

2. Think of someone you know who is suffering because his or her value system is not aligned with the Word of God. Then, pray a prayer of reconciliation over the situation.

3. Christ commented on the necessity of fasting when praying. (See Mark 9:29.) The power of prayer and fasting is nuclear! Participate in a fast, that you might dedicate a day, or a portion of a day, to prayer.

4. What questions do you have for God? Ask them freely, knowing that God has nothing but good in store for you and desires to reveal your destiny—through prophetic prayer! Ask and you shall receive, seek and you shall find, knock and the door will be opened.

About the Author

Pastor Kynan T. Bridges is the senior pastor of Grace & Peace Global Fellowship in Tampa, Florida. Through his profound revelation of the Word of God and his dynamic teaching ministry, Pastor Kynan has revolutionized the lives of many in the body of Christ. Through his practical approach to applying the deep truths of the Word of God, he reveals the authority and identity of the new covenant believer.

God has placed on Pastor Kynan a peculiar anointing for understanding and teaching the Scriptures, along with the gifts of prophecy and healing. Pastor Kynan and his wife, Gloria, through an apostolic anointing, are committed to equipping the body of Christ to live in the supernatural every day and to fulfill the Great Commission. It is the desire of Pastor Kynan to see the nations transformed by the unconditional love of God.

A highly sought speaker and published author of several books, including *Kingdom Authority* (Whitaker House, 2015), Pastor Kynan is also a committed husband, a mentor, and a father of four beautiful children: Ella, Naomi, Isaac, and Israel.

Welcome to Our House!

We Have a Special Gift for You

It is our privilege and pleasure to share in your love of Christian books. We are committed to bringing you authors and books that feed, challenge, and enrich your faith.

To show our appreciation, we invite you to sign up to receive a specially selected **Reader Appreciation Gift**, with our compliments. Just go to the Web address at the bottom of this page.

God bless you as you seek a deeper walk with Him!

WE HAVE A GIFT FOR YOU. VISIT:

whpub.me/nonfictionthx

WHITAKER
HOUSE